THE
Courtship
of GOD

A Journey of Love and Transformation

Jim & Shelvy Wyatt

Foreword by John Loren Sandford

5 Fold Media
Visit us at www.5foldmedia.com

The Courtship of God

Illustrated by Tom "T.J." Buchan, Cover Photography by Tim Maggio

ISBN: 978-1-936578-30-6

Library of Congress Control Number: 2012930966

Dedication

This book is dedicated to John and Paula Sandford, who imparted to us the foundations of our ministry and the mantle of Elijah. We value their ministry and their friendship.

To Betty and Fletch Fletcher, who were our mentors, counselors, and friends in the early days of our ministry as a couple.

Both couples lived their message before us.

Acknowledgments

We would like to thank Tom and Lora Maguire for their generosity and support. They serve faithfully on the intercessory board of our ministry.

Steve and Karen have blessed us with the use of their "cottage by the sea" on Prince Edward Island so we could have a quiet place to write; Jim and Kathy graciously opened their beach home in Rhode Island; Bruce and Sharon invited us to stay at their vacation home on the North Carolina shore.

We are so grateful for the continued support and encouragement of Susan Smith, Tom Maguire, and Christopher Cannon for reading the manuscript and giving us invaluable feedback. They serve on the board of directors of our ministry, as does Tom Buchan who did the illustrations. We wish to thank Steve and Sabrina Beane and Kathy Maggio for reading the manuscript, and Karen Wittwer for copy editing. Thanks to Stephen Sekeres for his encouragement in the writing of this book. To Leondra Bledsoe and Aimee Moore, thanks for their computer work; and a big thanks to Gillian Ridley for the excellent computer skills.

"Thank you" seems so inadequate for Lisa Leach who spent many hours editing. It was her idea to split up the original manuscript and make it a series of smaller books. This work is definitely enriched because of her input, such as the commentary on the Stations of the Cross. Blessings to you, Lisa!

Thank you, Tim Maggie, for the book cover photography. Kathy, thank you for fashion consulting, and to our model, Lindsay Blaze: You are beautiful inside and out, bless you!

To our Ghost Writer, the Author and Finisher of our faith, who made it all possible, we thank You, Jesus, for letting us live the adventure. May You receive all praise and honor!

Foreword

In *The Courtship of God*, Shelvy and Jim Wyatt have written a magnificent book. It will delight your heart with wondrous revelations, and in the same moment flay you alive, as the Holy Spirit shows you how far you are from living the simple truths Jim and Shelvy live routinely, every day.

Jim and Shelvy write alternately, sharing fascinating stories from their counseling sessions and from their own lives (without breaking confidentiality). They reveal how to use journals prophetically and for intercession. The process unfolds the major theme of the book—how our loving wonderful Father God uses everything in our lives to woo us to Himself, through our Lord Jesus Christ.

They teach, by sharing from their own lives, how to ponder what God may be doing in each event in our lives, events that we normally think of as too trivial to bother with. Along the way, they open our eyes to see the ever-present grace and providence of God. He is always there to love us—even in the pits of life. Valuable lessons about inner healing are to be learned in the many testimonial stories of people healed by counsel and prayer.

The Bible comes alive as they quote Scripture throughout the book. You will come away with regained hunger to continually delve into His Word.

Every opinion and statement in the book is documented scripturally, a valuable lesson in itself. Consequently, it would be difficult to find something to quarrel about theologically or biblically. The book is safe to read, but dangerous to complacency that often besets us all!

The Courtship of God purposefully does not tell a consecutive story. Shelvy and Jim jump from testimonies of healing, to stories of their own experiences, to chapters extolling the glory of God, to sermonettes exhorting us to rekindle our first love. This keeps us on our toes, not knowing what to expect next.

You will find yourself caught up in the process of having courtship with God, which is Jim and Shelvy's basic purpose in writing the book. May that be your experience! May you become unwilling to let anything deter you from responding to God's ever-loving courtship. I recommend reading and keeping the book nearby as a handy reference in the days and years to come.

Enjoy the book—and Him.

John Loren Sandford

Contents

Introduction

Have you ever thought about how God courts, woos, and expresses His love? He patiently pursues us like no other. We marvel at how the Lord of all Creation is also a very personal Admirer and Lover of our souls. His love is far greater than romance, as wonderful as that is. Our deep desire to be fully known, valued, understood, and affirmed can be answered by God better than any other; after all, He's the One who created that desire in us. He's also willing to wait until we're ready to receive more fully from Him. God loves us unconditionally, regardless of our ability to respond to Him. He plants clues for us throughout our lives, knowing that the time will come when we can finally begin to recognize them as the love notes that they are.

As a couple we were brought together by the Divine Matchmaker more than two decades ago. He used a prophetic dream to bring two broken people together for His purposes: our own healing as well as the healing of others. Come with us as we share wonders from our personal journey with you. It is a journey of His love and transformation. May your heart be transformed as you read on.

In this book we use the ancient art of storytelling. Uniquely threaded through each chapter are the testimonies of people we have had the privilege of encouraging through our ministry.

In most cases we have changed the names and identities. In some cases we have shown the most poignant of several peoples' stories that illustrate a particular message.

Can God's love reach into our past? We invite you to see how the Timeless One enables us to respond differently to our past through prayer and the renewing of our mind. Experience the transforming reality that you are God's own love-child, conceived in His heart and mind long before your birth. Perhaps you will identify with the stories of childhood wounds of rejection, abuse, abandonment, or sexual identity confusion. As you encounter these stories, embrace the Wonderful Counselor and Mighty Healer.

Perhaps you have felt that you've missed the nurture and freedom of childhood; you may have grown up with concerns and developed habits of performance or pressure to do the right thing at all times. It's not too late for the Lord to fill in those gaps so that your adulthood can be free of those old pressures and expectations.

We've found that having a healthy identity is essential to having an intimate relationship. Again, many have not had the kind of unconditional love that would help foster that healthy identity. Read how God tailors His calling to suit each person, speaking his or her love language in such a way that ushers in the transformation needed.

The book you're holding is the first of several in *The Courtship of God* series. We are currently finishing a volume on marriage, writing another about heavenly provision, and working on a fourth book concerning the mysteries of God. Look for these to follow, for they are all stories of God's great love for His children.

It is God's sacrificial love that causes Him to woo and choose us as His own. He has lovingly stepped into the circumstances of our lives to evidence Himself as our Protector and Provider, Savior and Deliverer. His love covers a multitude of sins and love never fails. Come receive His love and let it transform you forever. This is *The Courtship of God*!

Chapter 1: The Healing Power of Stories

As the big, black luxury car parked in front of my (Shelvy's) Christian bookstore, I wondered who the owner could possibly be. We just didn't see cars like that in the parking lot of our little strip shopping center of a half-dozen stores. The driver was a woman, fortyish, tall, and slender, dressed in tan slacks and a provocative black top. Her hair, a warm brown with blond streaks, was piled on top of her head. She slung a large handbag over her shoulder as she stepped out of the car and headed for the entrance to my store. She had a presence about her, like someone with authority. I smiled and greeted her, taking in a whiff of expensive perfume mingled with the smell of cigarettes.

"How may I help you?" I said.

Looking around, she replied, "Bibles, I want to see some Bibles."

I led the way to the Bible counter. Looking at the wall of shelves filled with Bibles, she seemed at a loss as to what to say. So I ventured forth, "Who is the Bible for, an adult or child?"

"Adult," came the husky reply.

Trying to narrow down the selection, I continued with another question. "Do you have a preference as to which translation?"

Her answer came quickly, "The Holy Bible." A pause. Then she said, "With the words of Jesus in red."

I felt that was enough questioning, I didn't want to add to her discomfort in what seemed like unfamiliar territory. I handed her one of the newer translations, moderately priced with a binding in imitation leather. She looked at it, turning it over in her hands. After she saw that the words of Jesus were in red, she said, "Do you have real leather?" I showed her the same Bible in genuine leather. She said, "I'll take three. Can I get the name printed in gold on the front?"

I was so curious about this unusual customer. I said, "If you have the time to wait, I'll be glad to imprint the Bibles now." She printed out the names for me, and I could see she had begun to relax a little. I invited her to sit down next to the worktable as I set the type for the imprinting. I asked, "Would you like us to gift wrap these for you?"

It was then the story came out. "No, gift wrapping won't be necessary." She continued, "One Bible is for me." She identified herself (I'll call her Ann). "One Bible is for my cook, and the other one is for one of my waitresses." I had to pray and ask the Lord to help me not mess up the imprinting because I was so enthralled with her story.

Ann owned a neighborhood bar. Three weeks earlier, she'd given her life to the Lord. She told me how she had given her life to the Lord, and how the first two weeks, she couldn't go near the bar; something just would not let her go there. I had finished the imprinting by then and I turned to her, giving her my undivided attention.

She could see the invitation to continue in my eyes, so the floodgates of information opened and spilled forth. She said, "I haven't known what to do. I know it's not right for me to drink anymore and I don't. But I feel a responsibility to my help; my cook has been with me eight years, and my girls, they need the work. I have a lease on the property. I can't just padlock the door indefinitely. And I have vendors to pay." She sighed and looked into my eyes to check out my reactions to her words. This woman was a woman of the "world." She had been around and knew how to read people. She continued, "The people in the church where I got saved say that if I'm really saved, I can't run a bar."

Everything in my spirit saw that this woman truly did know the Lord. I was overjoyed that she trusted me enough to share her heart with me. I was praying all along, *Lord, give me Your heart of love and wisdom for this woman.*

I said, "Would you like for me to pray with you and ask the Lord what you should do?"

"Oh, yes!" she responded, and bowed her head. As I prayed for her, I could sense the Lord saying, *Let your light shine.* And, *Bloom where you are planted.* After I shared that with her, she asked, "You mean, go back to the bar and keep it open?"

As contradictory as it sounds, I felt the Lord wanted Ann to go back to the bar and live her faith. Letting her light shine before those who knew her well seemed to be the message. She said her customers were mostly regulars who came in at the same time each week. I didn't know how this would work and line up with her new-found faith.

I opened the new Bible with her name on it and read to her from Philippians 4:6-7, "Be anxious for nothing, but in everything by prayer and supplication, with thanksgiving, let your requests be made known to God; and the peace of God, which surpasses all understanding, will guard your hearts and minds through Christ Jesus." I explained to her that as she prayed, God would tell her what to do and then she could apply the peace test.

I said, "Always, let the peace of Christ guard your heart and mind. If you don't have peace, then the Prince of Peace is saying, 'Wait, I'm not in this.'" Then I handed her a red pencil so she could underline these verses in her new Bible.

17

I assured her that I would be praying for her and invited her to come by anytime. In any way I could help, I wanted to be there for her. It was only a couple of days before Ann returned, this time armed with a plan. She had bought tracts by the hundreds. She selected several Christian movies to purchase about Moses and Jesus. She had a large screen television in the bar and when the games weren't on she planned to run the movies.

There were other times when Ann came by just to talk and pray. Her customers were hassling her, "You gone and got religion?" "What's the matter with you, you trying to turn this into some kind of church?" She said to me, "I think they think I'll get over it, but I can't get over what God has done for me. I can't keep quiet. What He's done for me, I want Him to do for them."

She also came in to buy more Bibles and always had the names of the people she purchased them for imprinted on the front cover. One by one, she took customers and employees to church with her. And she never seemed to tire of sharing her story.

One day, I heard her slam on the brakes of her car in front of the store and come running in while leaving the car engine running. One of "her girls"—that's what she called her waitresses—had overdosed and was in the hospital. Ann was on her way to the emergency room, and she was determined that this girl was not going to die without knowing the Lord. She was pulling out all the big guns in this battle for her soul. As she came running into the store, she said, breathlessly, "We have to pray; she just can't die!" I called all the employees and some of the customers gathered and we prayed and prayed. Then we sent her off, covered with the peace and assurance that the Lord had heard our prayers. Later that afternoon, Ann called. "She made it! They pumped out her stomach in time. She's going to live. Thank you for praying."

About six months had gone by since we first met. I had watched her grow unbelievably. She was so teachable that I just mentioned something to her and in her child-like faith she accepted it as the

18

truth, always asking where it was found in the Bible. She'd take out her red pencil and underline verse after verse.

Next time she came in with her sister, who was visiting from California. I noticed that Ann had shortness of breathe and was quite pale. She told me she was going into the hospital for open-heart surgery and the doctors had told her to go home and get her affairs in order. She knew her chances weren't good. We prayed and she had a contented look on her face. I commended her for the true evangelist that she was. I told her she had been obedient to God in letting her light shine; Ann truly had bloomed where He had planted her. I think she knew that this would be the last time we would see each other. I hugged her one more time.

She never came off the operating table.

Ann's first open-heart surgery was the spiritual kind, six months before when she opened her heart to receive Jesus Christ as her Lord and Savior. Now I could understand even more clearly why the Lord wanted her to keep the bar open. That's where she was known and those were the people who saw the change in her life. They saw her transformed by His love and their lives were touched as a result of the changes in her.

"You are the salt of the earth; but if the salt loses its flavor, how shall it be seasoned? It is then good for nothing but to be thrown out and trampled underfoot by men. You are the light of the world. A city that is set on a hill cannot be hidden. Nor do they light a lamp and put it under a basket, but on a lamp-stand, and it gives light to all who are in the house. Let your light so shine before men, that they may see your good works and glorify your Father in heaven" (Matthew 5:13-16).

Ann let her light shine and she was salty. She told me she used to "cuss like a sailor." But the Lord gave her the opportunity to be His salt, creating a thirst for the living waters of His Holy Spirit in those she encountered in her bar. She had developed a thick skin in order to survive the school of hard knocks. But that thick skin enabled her to take the ridicule and mocking and not yield to the temptation of people pleasing. She continued to share her faith right up to the end. Even as she told her customers and employees of her illness, it was not with anger and bitterness but with peace and a heart of gratitude for all He had done for her. Isn't that the true test of our faith—how we respond when things aren't going well?

Ann's story challenged those who came to her bar. From our childhood to old age, we love stories. Why? Because they open our hearts. Book, movie, television, or storyteller, it doesn't matter. As we envision someone else's story, we cry and laugh and it helps us to get in touch with our own story. We find that in many ways we are not so different after all; in story after story, we see that we share the need to love greatly and be loved greatly for who we are.

Jesus was a master storyteller and frequently spoke to people's situations with stories that illustrated hidden truths. About one-third of Jesus' teaching was in parables—brief stories from everyday life told to illustrate spiritual truths only available to those with open eyes to see and open ears to hear. Good stories are like that. They always have hidden truths to reveal to those who would seek them out. But stories can also relate lies to be accepted by the unwary or impure of heart to adopt as their "truth." Some movie writers change facts or history to promote the filmmaker's hidden agenda. It's important to discern God's truth in the midst of all the stories out there.

It's interesting to note that the Hebrew word for *truth* is "emeth."[1] It starts with the first character of the Hebrew

---

1. *Strong's Exhaustive Concordance*, s.v., H571, "emeth."

alphabet. Hebrew teachers believe this is significant in that "truth" encompasses all of creation, beginning to end. *Emeth* carries the idea of stability, certainty, or trustworthiness. You can place your confidence in it, with a surety. It is established, unwavering and dependable. It is a truth that transcends facts, yet withstands testing.

In the Gospel of Luke, seventh chapter, Jesus tells the story of a woman who had sinned much but also loved much. Jesus was invited to the house of the Pharisee, Simon. When the Pharisee did not extend to Jesus the common courtesies of the day, one would have to suspect that his motives weren't pure. Perhaps it was just curiosity that had caused him to open his house to Jesus. As the woman did what Simon hadn't done, Jesus said to his host, "Do you see this woman? I entered your house; you gave me no water for My feet, but she has washed My feet with her tears and wiped them with the hair of her head. You gave Me no kiss, but this woman has not ceased to kiss My feet since the time I came in. You did not anoint My head with oil, but this woman has anointed My feet with fragrant oil. Therefore I say to you, her sins, which are many, are forgiven, for she loved much. But to whom little is forgiven, the same loves little. Your sins are forgiven" (Luke 7:44-48).

The woman washing Jesus' feet was not unlike Ann. They had both sinned much but both loved much. I believe the influence of the woman who owned the bar exceeds many of us who have warmed the church pews for years. She couldn't keep her light hidden but shared her faith with all she encountered. How many have we led to the Lord? How many have we told of the transforming power of His love?

Prayer:

Father God, forgive me for the many times I have judged by what I saw with my eyes and heard with my ears. I have set myself up as judge, jury, and executioner—deciding who is guilty and what their punishment should be. I confess that I have a long list of "shoulds" and "ought-tos," and I measure others by those standards. I desire to be set free from any influence of a religious spirit. Forgive me, Lord, for my pride and arrogance, for I see that I have pushed You off the throne and I have seated myself in a god-like position. Lord, I see that my sin has created a barrier between You and me. Forgive me for grieving Your great heart of love. I humbly bow before You in repentance for my superior attitude toward others.

Only You, Lord, can look on the heart of man and know why he does what he does. Cleanse my heart, O God! Lord, You have a perfect will for each of our lives. You alone can look into the windows of our future and can see the completed landscape of our destiny. Thank You, Lord God, for being my Redeemer, for taking my messes and mistakes and weaving them into the fabric of Your love, thereby creating that which is the good, acceptable, and perfect will of God. Amen!

∽

Stories have the power to help us see with new eyes. We try on someone else's shoes and they take us out of our own mindset, beyond ideas and into the real-life world of another.

You can tell a man's beliefs by the stories he tells, the songs he sings, the jokes he laughs at, or the dreams he dreams. His stories are all based on the way he interprets truth. Truth doesn't change, but our interpretations do. The truth is that we don't see a thing as it is; we see it as we are. That is to say, we see through the filter of our values, our perceptions, and our beliefs about ourselves and the world around us. Our testimony is the story of Him who is the Truth working in each of our lives.

∽

A well-known alcohol recovery group was founded on the basis of shared experiences leading to healing and restoration. In the early days of this organization, a man found himself alone in a strange town and wanted to uphold his sobriety. He called a local pastor to arrange for him a meeting with a "known drunk." Upon meeting with the man, the drunk immediately told him how many had tried but couldn't reform him.

"No, you don't understand," the man said. "I'm not here for you; I'm here for me. I need your help." They then began to share the stories of their struggles.

Ask individuals who have attended group recovery meetings and they'll tell you it took them a while to recognize themselves in other's stories and to admit they were much the same. Yes, we're very different and unique in who we are and what we've experienced, but we're all cast in God's image. Built to love and be loved! Without it, all else is empty striving.

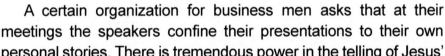

A certain organization for business men asks that at their meetings the speakers confine their presentations to their own personal stories. There is tremendous power in the telling of Jesus' work in their lives, men sharing their experiences with other men.

"One's own feelings and experiences of pain, fear, anger, guilt, shame, sadness, and joy can be a 'drawbridge' over which a communicator can carry the message and love of God into the deepest levels of people's lives."[2] When I (Shelvy) first read these words, I said "Lord, I want that to be my life and the life of this book, a 'drawbridge' to lead others into Your great arms of love."

---

2. J. Keith Miller: More Than Words (Baker Books), 70.

In the 1970s, Chaplain Ray had a fruitful prison ministry and radio program. He told of his attempts to hand out paperback books in the prison yard. The books were about God's saving work in reformed offenders' lives, and the men wanted no part of those "Jesus books" the preacher was touting. The chaplain was stuck with a boxful of books and no takers, until one of the prisoners said, "Give me that." He took the box from him and walked around the yard hawking, "Gangster stories for free!" The men quickly gobbled them all up. Of course they could relate to gangster stories—testimonies from their own kind![3]

Think about the sermons or lectures you may have heard. Do you remember them? If so, what stands out to you? Most often, it's the stories we remember. They are the keys that unlock revelations, a coming alive in our hearts and minds. The sermon is the hat rack, but the stories are the hats that we may try on for a moment. They're personalized, and we can keep those that fit us well. For a long time we cherish their warmth and closeness and can put them on again and again.

Consider the story that the Prophet Nathan told David. There was David, who had just committed some major sins and had added a cover-up to boot. If Nathan had simply told David what he'd done wrong, David may not have been open to it. After committing adultery with Bathsheba and finding his first attempt to cover it foiled, David had just given an order to place Uriah in the front line of battle to be killed. (2 Samuel 11-12). Uriah was one of David's mighty men, a faithful soldier and husband of Bathsheba.

When the Lord sent Nathan to David, he did not reprove him directly but began with this story: "There are two men in one city, one rich and the other poor. The rich man had exceedingly many flocks and herds. But the poor man had nothing, except one little ewe lamb that he bought and nourished; and it grew up together with him and his children. It ate of his own food

3. Chaplain Ray's International Prison Ministry, used with permission.

24

and drank from his own cup and lay in his bosom; and it was like a daughter to him.

"And a traveler came to the rich man, who refused to take from his own flock and his own herd to prepare one for the wayfaring man who had come to him; but he took the poor man's lamb and prepared it for the one who had come to him."

Upon hearing this, David's anger was greatly aroused and he vowed to punish the man. To which Nathan replied, "You are the man!" and proceeded to tell him the Lord's judgment against him. David then confessed, "I have sinned against the Lord." To which Nathan replied, "The Lord has put away your sin; you shall not die."

He then went on to tell David of God's judgment against him. If you read on it's interesting to note how quickly, like David, we judge another for having the same faults we have. We flare up on recognizing a weakness in someone else, which is really our weakness. We are all too ready, like David, to condemn another when we're guilty of the same offense. "Therefore you are inexcusable, O man, whoever you are who judge, for in whatever you judge another you condemn yourself; for you who judge practice the same things" (Romans 2:1).

We have wondered what might have been David's fate if he had repented upon hearing the story, without being so quick to judge another man's behavior? Nathan had to confront him because David's sin had blinded him. We can see another man's sin so much more easily than we can see our own. We all need a Nathan in our life, people who love us enough to speak truth when we need it and are blind to our sin. David said later, "When I kept silent, my bones grew old... Your hand was heavy upon me" (Psalm 32-3-4). To those who are not open to receive truth, a story is just another story. But for those who are willing, stories can bring truth to the mind and healing to the heart.

The Story of a Saving Army

My (Jim) story begins with the story of my mother. A story filled with heartache and hardship. One of my early memories was that my mother always had a love for the Salvation Army. However, it was years before I knew why. Mom became a devout Catholic convert at thirty years of age, before I was born. I suppose one reason she never said much about the Salvation Army was to avoid confusing our faith as children. It would be years later before I found out how much they had helped my mom in her earlier life. She'd sometimes stop at one of the Army's chapels in New York City to say a prayer while my younger sister, Joan, and I were with her. In the 1940s, this chapel was an inviting storefront sanctuary in the East Forties, off Broadway. From the sidewalk outside, you could see the full-length picture of Jesus glowing in red warmth, facing a double row of pews. The chapel was open to the public, but I don't remember seeing anyone but Jesus in there. It seemed to me He was there to welcome anyone who'd venture inside. That location has since changed to a newer facility to better meet the needs of theatre people on the west side of Broadway.

In 1904, my grandmother brought my mom, then age seven, and her sister, May, age nine, by ship to Ontario, Canada, from Plymouth, England. After many trials she had finally put an ocean between herself and her alcoholic husband, leaving him to work out his problems alone and to raise their older son, Howard. She worked as a registered nurse to earn a living (as did my mom and sister later on). But somehow tuberculosis, and the weight of it all, led to my grandmother's early death one year later. This left my mom and her sister as virtual orphans and wards of the state. They were fostered out separately to boarding homes and farms. In those days many of these were like indentured slave arrangements, the children being used as laborers: cooking, cleaning, and farming. The work was long and hard with little reward, recognition, or love. Their future looked like more of the same with not much to look forward to. Foster parents seldom had work or a place for more than one child. So my mom was separated from her older sister. Now she had no one. She missed her sister greatly. No one can know how much!

At sixteen, she was finally able to run away from the foster care system and pass as a grown up. She found work at Eaton's, a huge department store that covered a full city block in Toronto. She found a home with a kindly Catholic couple, the Mackeys, who rented her a room. They had a daughter, Jean, about mom's age, who soon became her best friend. The Mackeys treated her like a member of their family. Their lives reflected a loving influence that did much to inspire her to become a Catholic.

Meanwhile, Mom longed to find her sister May. She eventually sought out the Salvation Army's huge Missing Persons Bureau for help. The Salvation Army headquarters happened to be directly across the street from Eaton's store in Toronto. Mom had been working three years at Eaton's, in the cashier's department on the third floor, when she got a call from the Army to say they had found her sister. To her great surprise, she learned that May had been working at Eaton's for a little over a year as a salesgirl on the main floor. My mom had been going in the back entrance and her sister in the front entrance for over a year, never having occasion to see one another. Imagine her excitement as she raced down the stairs and onto the sales floor to once again see her sister's face. There was a tear-filled reunion right then and there. The floor manager gave them time to visit in the stockroom for as long as they needed.

The remembrance of that story still moves me. I can imagine the Lord's joy in orchestrating that reunion. He cares about our relationships with others as well as with Himself. An army of God's people had quietly worked behind the scenes doing His work to set love in order. I now understand more of what I didn't as a little boy. My mother's love for the Salvation Army was strong!

William Booth (1829-1912), founder of the Salvation Army wrote: "The chief dangers which confront the present century are religion without the Holy Spirit, Christianity without Christ, forgiveness without repentance, salvation without regeneration, politics without God, and heaven without hell. We are always in danger of following a form rather than a relationship, a method rather than belief and a quick fix rather than total death to our own righteousness so we might receive His." He understood the importance of reaching the heart and being truly changed in a personal way, by a very personal God.[4]

Did you know that the name *Jesus* means "God is my salvation"? Even His name stands for the truth that we can be saved only by God. *Christ* means "Anointed One." He came anointed and empowered with God's favor to bring the message of "God is my salvation." He then accomplished that truth in His death and resurrection.

It's interesting that the central chapter of all the chapters in the Bible, Psalm 118, has in its center, verse 14, "He has become my salvation." This is not a salvation that merely saves us from eternity in hell but an all encompassing salvation that covers spirit, soul, and body in the here and now. Salvation is so much more than our minds can comprehend, and it takes a lifetime to experience. Forgiveness, healing, prosperity, deliverance, and restoration are a few of the benefits of salvation. But the greatest of all is the opportunity to enter into a glorious, loving relationship

---

4. Found on a plaque at the Salvation Army building in Camp Connri, Ashford, CT. Used by permission.

with the Living God. That's what it's all about—Him becoming our very personal salvation each day of our lives.

We Are Part of His Story!

While each of us has our own story, there is a greater story being told and written in the heavenlies...His story = History! We are part of the greatest story ever told. It is the Story of a love so great that it could not be contained. God loves us so much that He gave His only Son to make a way for us to join our stories to His. The Lover of our souls wants us to spend every moment of every day, and then throughout eternity, with Him. Our God is writing a new message on our hearts. A message of sacrificial and unconditional love. It is the love of the Bridegroom as He draws us to Himself! Rest assured, Beloved, that although we don't know the last chapter of our story, it does have a happy ending!

Chapter 2: Divine Matchmaker

On March 27, 1985, I (Shelvy) awoke to the bright sunlight of Virginia Beach streaming through my bedroom window. I knew I'd just had a spiritual dream. I played the scenes over and over again before getting up and reaching for my journal. No human eyes looked upon my secret longings and dreams. Dreams of the daylight as well as those of the night were recorded there. Some were birthed out of pain and some not, but all given by the Lord.

I learned at an early age to take my dreams of the night seriously. I sometimes think God speaks to me in dreams so often because my mind and mouth are so busy during the day, He can't get a word in edgewise. Was this dream for the purpose of intercession, as many of my dreams have been, or was there more to it than that?

As I sat propped up on the bed pillows, I began to record the dream:

I was talking to a dark-haired man that I knew very well. I was sharing with him details about my trip to Israel last fall. He was listening intently as my excitement carried the telling. Then the sight of a little girl holding a camera in one hand distracted me. With her other hand she was trying to push her hair up into a knitted hat she wore. I went over to her and asked, "Honey, where's your mother?"

She replied, "My mother died and she's in heaven with Jesus."

31

"My children's father died and he's in heaven, too," I told her. Then I said, "Let me help you fix your hair." As I took off her hat and started twisting her hair up to be covered better, I felt someone's eyes on us. I looked up and saw a tall, handsome man with salt-and-pepper gray hair, wearing a light blue sweater and watching protectively over the little girl. Assuming that possibly he was her father, I continued helping her. Again, I felt the eyes upon us. But this time as I looked up, I saw the same man with three or four men standing around him, talking. He had his arms crossed over his chest and I felt that he needed to be loved to life. Now, I noticed for the first time, a younger man, dark hair, seated at my right and working with his hands. He wasn't watching any of us, but I knew he was observing everything that was going on. That was the end of my dream.

I felt a burden to pray for the little girl and the tall, handsome man. It's not unusual for me to pray for people I don't know. In fact, I know they may be representative of someone, somewhere and I simply need to lift them up to the Lord. The burden was especially heavy that morning as I went to the Christian bookstore that I owned. After greeting my dear friends and loyal employees, Dot and Minna, I shared the dream with them. I stayed in my office most of the morning, interceding as I felt the Spirit lead me. Over the next three or four days, the call to pray came in waves, sometimes in the middle of the night.

I shared these things with a group of young wives of military men with whom I met each week to teach the Bible. It was such a privilege to impart to these wives and mothers the riches of the Word and the ways of the Lord in a mentoring relationship. It was like preparing missionaries, as they would be traveling the world while their husbands served our nation in faraway places. Since reading *Trauma of Transparency,* my life had become an open book[5]. Once a week, I also led a home group for several

---

5. Howard Grant, Trauma of Transparency, (Multinomah: 1979).

couples. They had become like family to me, especially since my husband died. So, it was quite natural to share the dream with them as well. On Sunday mornings, I taught a couples Sunday school class. Once again, I told the dream and then asked them to intercede in prayer with me. As a teacher, I believe God hasn't just called me to impart knowledge but that my entire life is a teaching. So it isn't unusual for me to share whatever is going on in my life.

After all that telling and a few days had gone by, life went on and I forgot all about the dream. However, the Lord, Who goes before us, had a purpose in it all. Our prayer is that as you read of how the Lord used that dream, your faith will be built, as was the faith of all those with whom the Lord had us share this story.

A couple months later, a surprise phone call came one night from a dear woman, Margaret. I had met her on my trip to Israel in September of 1984. She was recovering from a near-death experience from a brain aneurysm, and surgery. She said she had a lot of time to think about her future and was interested in pursuing another master's degree. She wanted to check out a Christian university in Virginia Beach. I offered her a place to stay at my home. A couple more months went by, then Margaret called again. Her plans were to drive down from her home in Connecticut with the help of two people from her church. One of her friends was an older woman, and the other was a man in his early 50s, who was in the process of becoming a priest. They were to arrive on August 6, 1985.

Since the death of my husband in February 1984, I had made an inner vow that I would never, ever get married again. I had been hurt enough and had put up a wall a mile high to protect myself. It was just me and the Lord. I said to the Lord, *I pulled my time and received an early parole from a life sentence. Thank you, Lord it's over! I'm free, and I'm going to stay that way!*

I know that sounds awful, but that is where I was at the time. Those statements reveal a lot of hurt but also a lot of sinful reactions. From my lifetime as a Protestant, I thought all priests remained single, so I wasn't concerned about meeting Margaret's friend, the would-be priest. For a week before they arrived, I read Madam Guyon's book, *Experiencing the Depths of Jesus Christ*[6] and I felt I should fast while doing so. It is a life-changing little book and it had quite an impact on me. Unbeknownst to me, God had His purposes, one of which was to deal with my fears by ministering the reality of His love. "Perfect love cast out fear" (1 John 4:18).

"Fear is the dark room where our negatives are developed."[7]

On August 6, Margaret and her two friends arrived in Virginia Beach. When I first met Jim, I thought he looked familiar, but after some conversation it appeared that our paths had never crossed. I had never been to Connecticut and he had never been to Virginia Beach.

Jim's Perspective

When I first met Shelvy, she had come off the elevator on the fourth-floor balcony of a hotel in Virginia Beach. It was a high and breezy place and I was waiting outside the rooms of the two lady friends. I knew a little about her from Margaret's telling of their Israel tour. I knew she owned a bookstore where she counseled many, drawing inspiration and instruction from the books of John and Paula Sandford. I had studied their work and even taught some from their first books. I believe I first saw Shelvy as a woman of substance, to be honored for her giving to many. (It was how

---

6. Madam Guyon, *Experiencing the Depths of Jesus Christ*, (Christian Books Publishing 1975).
7. Original author unknown.

Boaz must have felt about Ruth when he first saw her, although I didn't think about Boaz at that time.)

We all said our hellos and Shelvy took us to dinner at one of those fun restaurants with an eclectic décor. There were all kinds and sizes of memorabilia filling the floors, walls, and ceilings: a large red British phone booth, a tuba, airplane, canoe, and much more. Eating booths were placed in an elevator, a prison cell, a Ferris wheel seat, and a four-poster bed. The hostess chose to seat us in the eagle's nest, which was up the stairs and then up another spiral staircase into the third-level rafters. It was so much fun being able to look down on all that was going on in the restaurant from our high perch.

This began a conversation about eagles. We found we both shared a love for eagles. Both of us had taught for years about the spiritual metaphors to be found in eagles. I talked about my eight-year membership in a Connecticut Soaring Club, where I learned to soar as an eagle does. The club's power plane would tow me up thousands of feet in one of the club's sailplanes and release the tow to enable me to soar. I'd look for potential updrafts to catch and circle in to rise higher and remain airborne longer, just as an eagle does when he mounts up on air currents. I shared how much it was like catching the wind of the Spirit and letting Him take you up higher. I had been endeavoring to follow the gentle urging of the Holy Spirit for years. Shelvy later said she was thoroughly impressed.

Spirit Eagle

I (Shelvy) was delighted to hear Jim talk of his experience in the soaring club. The more he talked, the more it became evident that he was an "eagle Christian." One wall in my office was covered with pictures and plaques of eagles. Many were given to me because I had given a teaching about the spiritual parallels in the life of an eagle from Isaiah 40:31. It has to do with waiting on the Lord and mounting up with eagle's wings. It is an active seeking after that which you can only see with eyes of faith. An eagle knows they will find uplifts of air even though they can't see them. That's his faith. He knows the habits of air and searches accordingly. But he still can't physically see what he is seeking. When the eagle physically senses an uplift of one wing tip, he turns and circles in it. He has learned to sense that which he cannot see. The eagle has learned to immediately obey those uplifts as he actively waits. So we, too, are to be waiters (servers) on the Lord—constantly watching as bondservants, watchmen for the wind of the Spirit.

My Connecticut guests returned home, and I thought that was the last time I would see Jim. The Lord had used this experience to continue His healing and refining in me. As my protecting walls were coming down and I was responding to the convicting power of the Holy Spirit to repent of my inner vows, something was happening to my heart. At first, I thought, *the Lord just wanted me to know that there are some godly men out there. After all, this one has gone back to his home in Connecticut and there is no reason to think that I will ever see him again*...but God had other plans!

Working my way through a stack of mail, I was surprised to see an envelope postmarked from Connecticut. It was a thank-you note from Jim. He was thanking me for my kindness in showing them around Virginia Beach, treating them to dinner, and the book, *Experiencing the Depths of Jesus Christ*. That started me thinking about him again.

Margaret decided to move to Virginia Beach to go to school there. She said she would have to rent a truck to move her stuff. I volunteered our family van, which had remained in my garage since my husband's death. I was happy for it to be of some use to her. So Margaret and I drove the van up to Connecticut.

"A woman is like a tea bag, she doesn't know how strong she is until she's in hot water." -Former First Lady, Eleanor Roosevelt[8]

A Dream Come True

It was while in Connecticut that Margaret and I were walking up the aisle at her church when I looked up and saw Jim standing with his arms crossed over his chest and three or four men standing around him talking.

For the first time since meeting Jim, my mind was triggered to remember the dream. That was a scene from the dream, where three or four men were talking with the tall, handsome man. Now I understood why he seemed so familiar. He was the man in the dream! I grabbed Margaret's hand and said, "I've got to tell you something!" So we went outside and I told her all about the dream. She asked, "When did you have this dream?" I looked in my journal and said, "March 27, 1985." She got an amazed look on her face and excitedly said, "That was the morning I was having brain surgery! I am the little girl you were praying for!"

Then she went on to explain that Jim was at the hospital keeping her two sons company while she was in surgery. She said, "I know it may sound vain, but I was so upset that they had to shave all my hair off for the surgery." So it seemed God had more than one reason for giving me that dream. He was introducing me to Jim and letting me know our meeting was of Him. And He had me praying for my little friend who is less than five feet tall and who was head mistress for a children's school she had founded. She has authored two books and when we were in Israel together she always had her camera in hand. She was definitely the little girl in my dream. It would be months later

---

8. Eleanor Roosevelt, *You Learn by Living*, (Louisville, KY: Westminster John Knox Press, 2009).

before I would find out that there was yet another reason God gave me the dream when He did.

After loading her stuff in the van, Jim said he would drive it back to Virginia Beach with me and then fly back home. The first time Jim and I were ever alone was in that van. We had been on the road a short time when Jim began to tell me about a dream he'd had the night before. He said, "There was a dark-haired man in my dream and I'm sure he represented Jesus."

When he finished telling the dream, I said, "A few months ago I had a dream with a dark-haired man in it; I wonder if he represents Jesus also. Could I tell you the dream and see what you think?" I told him the dream but did not mention Margaret and her surgery or any other interpretation. He listened intently, and then said, "The dark-haired man you were talking with about your trip to Israel is Jesus. The little girl is Margaret." Then he started laughing. I asked, "Who do you think the tall, handsome man is?" He answered through his laughter, "It's me!"

We saw the hand of God in our meeting and maybe we would become friends. Jim had been divorced for ten years. He had gone through repentance for leaving his wife and had asked for reconciliation but was told by his former wife that she wasn't interested. She had met someone else and remarried six days after the day he sought reconciliation with her (though he didn't know about that at the time). Through his midlife crisis ten years ago, Jim had come to know the Lord in a personal way. It wasn't that he was against getting married again; Jim just wanted to make sure it was God's will.

We enjoyed the couple of days together, traveling to Virginia Beach and helping Margaret get her things settled in her new condo. But when Jim flew back to Connecticut, I really thought that would be the last time I would see him. I was thankful to the Lord for showing me that I could be friends with a godly man and not be afraid of being hurt. I could just relax and be myself. Even though I found out the kind of priest he was becoming was one who could marry.

Through this brief experience, something was happening in my heart. It was becoming soft and pliable rather than hard and rigid. I began to think maybe it was possible for me to have a healthy relationship with a man. Hope began to rise up in my heart and mind. Now there was a mixture of fear and desire for my future. I decided to go on another fast for God to purify my heart and make me more willing to say, "Your will, not mine be done!"

Once again, I did a lot of repenting. I remember at my niece's wedding, I was seated at the reception with several couples that were dear friends of their family. When one of my sisters introduced me as a widow, one well-meaning lady said, "We'll just have to pray for you for a new husband." I almost bit her head off by saying, "Please don't—I don't want to be married again!"

Then I remembered when I was on a trip to Israel with dear friends, John and Paula Sandford. We were at a threshing floor and John read the scripture from the Book of Ruth and explained how they threshed the wheat at that time. Someone in our group said, "Shelvy, you are our young widow like Ruth. Why don't you stand by the threshing floor so we can get a picture." I replied, "I'll be glad to stand there but just make sure there is no Boaz in the picture!" After the picture taking, John said to me, "Shelvy, you come and sit with me on the bus. You and I have some things to talk about." I knew by the look on the face of this man, who was like a spiritual father to me, that I was in for some correction. My bitterness was showing and he was right to tell me so. He said to me, "The day you gave your life to the Lord, you gave up the right to say, 'No Boaz in the picture!'" Then he lowered the bomb, "And furthermore, God is going to send you a husband!" Not exactly what I wanted to hear. But I knew God wanted my willingness and that was all I could contemplate at that time.

When I was back home, John and Paula called me saying, "What is going on with you? You have been on our hearts for the past three weeks." I answered, "A few weeks ago I met a man and I can't stop thinking about him. It would take me a couple of hours to tell you all about it." John said, "We are going to be up the coast from you in a couple of weeks. Why don't you fly up and spend some time telling us all about it." I heard myself asking, "Where are you going to be?" John informed me that they were going to be in a conference in Darien, Connecticut. I almost shouted in excitement, "That's where the man lives! In Connecticut!" Now I really began to believe God was up to something.

I determined I would not let Jim know I was coming to Connecticut. If God was doing something, He didn't need my help. Besides, I needed God to do it. I didn't trust myself. Maybe all this was my own imagination. Margaret knew I was going up to spend time with John and Paula and that I would be staying at a hotel in Greenwich. She told a friend who told Jim. But I didn't know any of this at that time.

The night before I flew up to Connecticut, I asked the Lord to speak to me through the Bible because I didn't trust the impressions in my mind. This is a terrible thing to admit for a teacher of the Bible, but it reflects my desperation for God's will. I closed my eyes, held my Bible with both hands, and then let the pages fall open wherever they would. I looked at the top of the page and read, "Wives submit to your own husbands, as to the Lord." I said, "Lord, I had more than twenty years of that!" The Lord said to my heart, *Keep reading.* I continued reading from Ephesians 5:22-33. When I got to verse 29, it was like the words jumped off the page at me, "nourishes and cherishes." The Lord said to me, *I have sent Jim into your life to be your husband and he will nourish and cherish you!* I could only reply, "Tell him!"

The next day I flew up to Connecticut from Virginia Beach. I knew I would not be seeing John and Paula until the following day, so I changed my clothes, put on a comfortable jumpsuit, and was barefoot. I did not plan on seeing anyone. Much to my surprise, the telephone rang and it was Jim. He said, "I heard you were in town for the Sandfords' conference. I was supposed to have a clergy meeting tonight but it has just been canceled. How about I come over to see you, and maybe we could have dinner?"

During the short time before Jim arrived, I prayed, "Lord, bring to death all these thoughts I've been having about this man. Just let me be myself, like I would be with any friend."

I opened the drapes to the large picture window that opened to the terrace, and we sat and talked. We had not seen or heard from each other in a month. He had a granddaughter born during that time. Both of my children were off in college. We enjoyed sharing what was going on in each of our lives. When he asked what God was doing in my life, I swallowed hard and said, "God has been showing me my bitterness and sinful inner vows, and He is asking me to be willing to be married again. He gave me Ephesians 5 concerning that." I reached for my Bible and read the Ephesians scripture without any comment on my part.

When I finished the reading, Jim said, "Excuse me." He got up and went into the bathroom. I didn't think anything of it, I just thought he was using the facility. But, was I in for a surprise when he returned with a towel over one arm and carrying the white wastepaper basket filled with warm soapy water. He knelt at my feet and said, "The Lord told me to wash your feet."

I had never seen foot washing, although I knew it was in the Bible and that there are some churches that practice that tradition. It was the most humbling experience I have ever had. It was like having Jesus kneeling at my feet. The Word of God was pouring out of him and my heart was flying ninety miles an hour. My mind went to the Ephesians 5 scripture that said the husband was to wash his wife with the water of the Word. I didn't say a word about that, but to me, Jim was performing a prophetic act and this was a confirmation to what the Lord had said to me the night before about Jim being my future husband. After he washed my right foot, he placed it on the towel and bent forward and kissed the top of my foot! I thought I was going to be raptured on the scene. It was so very intimate! Then he did the same thing with the other foot. I was speechless!

After he returned the basin and towel to the bathroom, Jim sat across from me and explained, "While you were reading scripture, the Lord told me to wash your feet. I said, 'Huh?' So the Lord repeated it, 'Wash her feet' and I knew I was to be obedient." He said he felt he was to wash my feet as Jesus did the disciples, as I was a woman the Lord used as a minister to many." God wanted me to honor you." We interpreted this whole event differently, but that was God's business. The next day, I shared all of this with John and Paula. They listened and prayed with me.

Jim's View

When I found myself with an open schedule, having heard previously of Shelvy's early arrival for the Sandfords' conference, I dialed her room and found myself suggesting we have dinner together. Upon seeing her, we shared some of the happenings in our lives, discussed some books and listened to several tapes she had brought. We found that we both loved the same song about eagle's wings. It was such a moving song, honoring someone who had been uplifting like the wind, and we both felt it was about Jesus.

Shelvy asked if she could read the Scripture from Ephesians the Lord had given her the night before and explained how she felt the Lord was asking her to be willing to marry again. In the midst of her reading, the Lord spoke directly to me the words, *Wash her feet.* My thought was, *Huh?* He merely repeated, *Wash her feet.* As I moved to obey, I reasoned that I was to honor her as Jesus did the disciples. Like theirs, her feet were unclean from walking in the world (ministering) though she was clean all over. I didn't know until later the greater significance from the Ephesians passages she had just read. Husbands are to be as Christ with His bride and to cleanse their wife with "the washing of water by the Word." The Lord is always doing greater things than we realize. We obey out of limited knowledge, while He works His unlimited goodness.

He began a mighty work in me but very different to what He was doing in Shelvy. First of all, she believed that the Lord was to have me be her husband, while I was unaware of this. I believe the Lord began to strengthen me and draw me closer to Him in His love…to free me from any fears I might have in committing that love to Shelvy. He never told me "I want you to marry Shelvy." No, rather, he brought her to me with evidences of His presence as a loving Father in those meetings. I realized that this was my commitment to make and my choice to decide. In a marriage the man commits and the woman receives that commitment, just as it is with Christ and His Bride.

As an instance of God's strengthening presence, God gave me a vision the first night of the conference. Shelvy and I were standing together during a time of prayer and song at the opening of the meeting. All our hands were lifted in praise when something touched my hand. I opened my eyes and saw nothing nearby. Shelvy's hands fully raised are about a foot below mine, so it wasn't her. I closed my eyes again and felt impressed to ball up my raised hands. As I did I saw in my mind's eye two large eagle's claws surround and grip my hands. I was then lifted as in a dark airshaft, rising higher. I could feel the air blowing by, though there was no air in the natural. I thought to myself, *I'm going to see heaven, the kingdom.* In a moment the Lord said, *Open your eyes. This is the kingdom.* I did and saw all those at the conference around me. The Lord gave me the interpretation in Exodus 19:4: "How I have bore you on eagle's wings and brought you to Myself." I understood how He had lifted me up out of the darkness and brought me to His people…out of the sewer and into the light.

We sat down after this to hear the conference coordinator announce a special addition. A soloist friend, Joyce, would sing and play keyboard for us. She performed the same eagle's wings song that Shelvy and I both loved, and I lost it completely in quiet tears of joy. You could have knocked me over with a feather (pun intended). Both Shelvy and I recognized the Lord's hand in all this, manifesting His love for us. We had listened to that song only the night before. I told Shelvy later that I knew the Lord had brought us together for His purposes and that I was committed to whatever He was doing.

It was platonic, and Shelvy was seeing my wariness at this point. I was making no moves that I felt the Lord wasn't in, but I had confidence that His will would be accomplished. Shelvy, however, was more expectant in light of God's statement to her and all that God was doing. Over the previous years, several women friends had disclosed to me their expectations of marrying me, which they claimed the Lord had told them. Usually these pronouncements took me by surprise. "It's the Lord's will that we marry and have (some) great ministry together." None of these ladies had even been so much as kissed by me for my fear of unintentionally leading them on. At one point I had vowed to the Lord never to love again except under His leading. I hadn't had a desire for years to pursue anything but friendships. Such friendships were usually formed as part of some group gathering or work. I was cautious about any dating or pairing off in any exclusive way. (For example, I regret accepting one woman's invitation to Sunday dinner at her home after church. I was naïve to the inferences she would draw from my friendly acceptance.)

I've asked myself why these women were drawn to me so frequently in their loneliness or hurt. The Lord has shown me an unredeemed natural compassion that I have for wounded women that resulted from seeing my mother's pain and rejection during my dad's drinking years. I desired to help and comfort her but in my childhood was unequipped to do so. That was my father's role. But I took on the shame and guilt of that. This left me with a sense of inadequacy. Only Jesus can remove that stigma and give me His true compassion for others and myself. We are to desire for people to be drawn to Him and His compassion in us. Jesus is the only one who can truly heal.

When I asked Shelvy to dinner, I felt completely at peace in doing so. I had learned to give the Lord my will each day so I would be guided by His perfect peace. I endeavor to trust in His guidance in all my desires and questions each day. Then He is able to direct my paths without my asking permission at every turn.

During the first evenings of the conference, Shelvy was thinking that perhaps she had made a mistake in coming, because of my unresponsiveness to what she saw God doing. I believed she would remain unless the Lord willed differently. She questioned me to see if I could comprehend all God was doing, without ever divulging the Lord's pronouncement that I was to be her husband. We had some good conversations. God was working in both of us. I was talking to the Lord and wrestling with many questions.

By Saturday afternoon, when I arrived at the conference, I sat beside Shelvy in the rear pews and greeted her with "Hello, Ruth." She blushed. She knew something had changed. I knew that calling her by that name was indicating to her that I saw her as more than a woman of worth. Later that evening I told her that I believed that the Lord had brought us together as a couple and that I was committed to whatever He was doing with us.

Shelvy's View

When I went to the meeting on Saturday, and Jim came in and sat beside me saying, "Hello, Ruth," I got the feeling that God was really enjoying all of this. I knew God had been dealing with Jim when he said he was committed to us as a couple. I went to Jim's church for the Sunday worship service and his pastor came out and said, "I'm not going to deliver the sermon I had prepared for

45

he Courtship of God

today. This morning the Lord told me to speak to you on Ephesians 5." Then he proceeded to read the same passage of scripture the Lord had given to me the night before I flew up to Connecticut for the conference. Then he exhorted the men, "Just as Jesus washed the feet of the disciples, you husbands are to wash the feet of your wives. You are to wash them with the water of the Word." I felt this was another confirmation of what the Lord had spoken to me but I didn't say anything. I later wrote it all down in my journal. I wanted to keep my heart and mind straight before God.

The Lord kept doing things that I couldn't call a coincidence. He was being so tender with me to give me confirmations. He was dealing with Jim in a different way. I believe the biblical position of the woman is to be open and receptive to the man. But, the man's position is to commit. And commit he did! On Monday morning Jim came to me and said, "I believe the Lord has brought us together for the purpose of marriage and I'm committed to that."

I responded in typical female fashion. "Well, ask me!" I didn't want him to ever say, "I only married her because God told me to." While I knew he was following God's leading, I wanted him to also choose me for himself. You women readers understand what I'm talking about.

On October 14th, we became betrothed. We didn't call it engagement because we knew God had arranged this whole thing. Our part was to be obedient to fulfill all God's purposes for bringing us together. Here we were, the first time we ever met was August 6, and now, it's October 14th and we are betrothed. For most of those seventy days, I was in Virginia Beach and Jim was in Connecticut. We had been together less than a dozen times. But we had both walked with the Lord a lot of years and we knew His ways. And this was His doing. We prayed together and asked the Lord when He wanted us to marry. I felt that it had to be after January 11th, because that was when my daughter, Sabrina, was getting married to Steve Beane, a wonderful young man she met while attending college. During this time I was planning her wedding and reception. We got out our calendars for the coming year, 1986. We had commitments in February but March was wide open. Jim noticed that Easter came the last Sunday of March that year, and he said, "How would you like to honeymoon in the Holy Land and be over there for Resurrection Sunday?" We both have a love for Israel. Jim had gone there on a sixteen-day tour in 1979 and several years later had spent a short time studying at the Institute of the Holy Land in Jerusalem. Before we met, I had visited the Holy Land on a tour with John and Paula.

As we talked, we began to dream of possibly marrying in Israel. Further, we wondered, wouldn't it be wonderful to be married on a mountaintop—where eagles dwell—at sunrise? As we talked of the mountaintops we had visited, I expressed my delight in Mount Tabor. The Basilica of the Transfiguration is a beautiful church built on top of the mountain along with a monastery. It is the traditionally accepted site of the Transfiguration of Jesus.

The place where I (Shelvy) experienced the presence of the Lord more than any other was the Mount of Transfiguration (Mt. Tabor). It is off the beaten track and a lot of tourists don't go there as it is far from the other tourist attractions. The Franciscan brothers of the Catholic Church have built a monastery on top of that mountain and the only way up is a narrow, winding road that zigzags back and forth with thirty hairpin turns. It is worth the effort, for the church has magnificent mosaics of angels on the walls leading up to the altar and breathtaking stained glass windows behind the altar. So we decided to investigate that possibility. Jim put in a call to John and Paula to see what their availability was to marry us in March while they would be leading a tour in Israel. And when would they be at Mount Tabor?

He called me at my home in Virginia Beach. "John and Paula are leading the Israel tour March 17th through March 27th. They have a full itinerary every day except the last day, which is when they'll be at Mount Tabor. John says he can marry us on Thursday, March 27th at sunrise."

I could hardly believe my ears. I couldn't hold back the tears. I cried into the telephone, "Jim, don't you realize what that date is?"

He said, "Sure, it's Holy Thursday before Easter."

I came back through tears of joy, "No, no, that is the date of the dream where I first saw you, March 27th!" The Lord was being so very gracious to us by confirming once again that He had arranged this marriage from beginning to end. It was all His doing. He gave me the dream on March 27th as a way of preparing me to meet Jim. He wanted me to know it was Him ordering my steps and He didn't want me to be afraid. Now He had arranged for us to marry on that exact day one year later on the Mount of the Transfiguration. What a privilege to be married there!

We made the necessary calls and arrangements for our wedding to take place on March 27th, in the Church of the Transfiguration on Mt. Tabor, Israel. Before the wedding date, we had a reception in Greenwich, CT, for all of Jim's family and friends. And we had another reception in Virginia Beach for all of my (Shelvy's) family and friends. There was much rejoicing, for many had been with us through the tears of sorrow, and now they were with us for the tears of joy.

Jim decided to make our wedding rings. He wore a gold ring he bought from a jeweler on Jaffa Street in Jerusalem. His ring had the Hebrew letters spelling, "Yeshua." I wore a silver ring with the letters ICHTHUS, the Greek word for "fish," which is also the Christian symbol. Its letters abbreviated the acronym for Jesus Christ, Son of God, Savior. I am reminded of a quote from Randy Alcorn's book *Safely Home*: "Real gold fears no fire!"[9] For it was his plan to put our rings in the fire as God was about to do with our lives.

---

9. Randy Alcorn,*Safely Home* (Carol Stream, IL: Tyndale House, 2001), 149.

Rings of Love

What is a ring? A ring is a circle, a surround that encloses and protects. It can mean continuing cycles of repetition, coming back to the beginning and a permanence of unity within. A ring is also a symbolic encirclement enclosing and retaining its wearer in an "office," or position they or another has chosen or had designed for them. Rings are worn to convey a statement. The wearer has covenanted with or committed to some belief or truth they wish to convey symbolically. Whether it's the regent wearing a seal of his office or a lady with a large diamond simply saying, "I'm prosperous," the ring speaks.

Why wear a ring? Some take on these symbols of covenants hoping that the very taking will somehow cause or magically guarantee an illusive hoped for reality. A person wearing a fraternity ring might be saying, "I am everything honorable this group stands for." Others disdain their symbols, desiring a freedom of sorts that doesn't exist. I'm thinking of the man who won't wear a wedding band because It might catch in machinery, and yet he works in an office. We are deceived by commitments to false beliefs. If we practice to deceive others then we are ultimately deceived and lose control of our own lives. Just as some will wear or not wear rings to project a nonexistent fantasy, others will wear a ring to portray a truth that exists or is hoped for in their lives. Symbols can be powerful in conveying a truth that is difficult to convey in words. Symbols came before words were written. The first words were symbols or pictures. All words are symbol pictures of something we have in mind. We hope and trust others will see what we see in the symbol.

When we seek to convey truth, if we have given control over to Jesus, we will find true freedom. At the beginning and the end He is the truth we are all seeking.

We have both worn rings and made covenants like all of the above. Let us tell you the story of our wedding rings and the rings that led up to them...an adventure in the Lord's transforming love. I, (Jim) had worn a ring for years that a friend had given me when she discovered it in a Greenwich Village artisan's shop. It was a crafted gold band in the image of the Egyptian "Eye of Horah," the sun god. It looked like the eye image you'd see on the hieroglyphic walls of a tomb in an Indiana Jones-type movie. She said it was a symbol of health, wealth, and prosperity. *What a nice gift...so unique...who doesn't want health, wealth and prosperity!* I thought as I began wearing it.

As the years went by and I was experiencing a greater "God consciousness," I rationalized more and more that the ring was a symbol of the all-seeing eye of God, like a symbol of Father God. A good Christian friend who I respected said, "I don't know, Jim," but left it at that. He knew our God was big enough to work it out with me.

One night in 1979, I was studying my Bible while sitting on a small bench on Mount Zion in Jerusalem, overlooking the Gehennah Valley (facing toward Egypt, as it turns out). I had come to take a short course in biblical geography. Under a small light bulb outside the school's walls, I happened to be reading Deuteronomy chapters 7 and 8 and was convicted by the words about graven images. I made a quick decision, removed the Egyptian ring, crushed it underfoot, and threw it out over the valley into the darkness it came from. God knew His holy mountain was a fitting place to separate me from a symbol of my idols of health, wealth, and prosperity.

The next day, I walked up to a jewelry shop on Jaffe Street, the main shopping avenue in Jerusalem, to purchase a "Yeshua" (Jesus) ring to replace it, a simple gold band with the Hebrew characters for Jesus' name emblazoned on it. Thereafter, I wore this ring, with the name of the true Prince of Peace. Much later I realized that this word "peace" that Jesus spoke to the disciples was the Hebrew "shalom." It signifies so much more than we usually consider. In its fullness it conveys the tremendous well being that He has come to bring, the abundant life, health, wealth, and prosperity the Lord would give—not as the world gives, as was symbolized in my discarded ring.

This peace is only found in Him. To attain it we must throw away all the idols we covenant with, even giving away our own life for His sake in order to find our life, our rest, in Him. "For whoever desires to save his life will lose it, but whoever loses his life for My sake will find it" (Matthew 16:25). Just as I, after throwing away the ring, entered into the walled city of Peace (Jerusalem) to rest that night.

I, (Shelvy) had purchased the silver Ichthus ring years before and now wore it on my left hand instead of the right as I had formerly, to replace my wedding band when my husband died in 1984. It was similar to a wedding band in appearance and served to keep me separate from any potential suitors, my heartfelt desire at that time.

When we covenanted to marry (became betrothed), one of the common threads of our separate ministries had been Isaiah 40:31, "But those who wait on the Lord shall renew their strength; they shall mount up with wings like eagles, they shall run and not be weary, they shall walk and not faint." We had both used the eagle as a metaphor to teach God's principles and we had each collected stories, pictures, and music about them.

So I, (Jim) envisioned wedding bands in the form of an eagle's nest. Eagles take one partner for life. What "God has joined together let no man put asunder." For our marriage to fly we knew it would have to rest on the winds of the Holy Spirit. We knew that with God all things are possible. As we rested in obedience to

His guidance, He could overcome the difficulties of our past and purify us from our old sinful ways.

So I fashioned rings in beeswax to the exact shape and design we desired. I first fashioned many sub-miniature branches and twigs of varying configurations, then I wove them together on the two appropriately sized mandrels for Shelvy and me, into the wedding-band master patterns. I had developed a jewelry-making skill as a hobby during the years before this. A goldsmith would later cast these in gold. Using what's called the "lost wax process" the goldsmith was able to make molds and then gold rings to exactly duplicate these wax masters. We each contributed our "Jesus rings" and some other old gold to the melt. The goldsmith added new gold to bring the gold karat weight up, poured our new rings and then finished, sized, and polished them—eagle's nest rings befitting a mountaintop wedding.

The mixing of these remnants of each of our individual lives in Christ with the new was a perfect symbol of our new corporate lives. Silver represents redemption, while gold the divine. The two are a model of our lives and our marriage as redeemed in Christ and corporate in Him. Just as we are totally established in Christ when we surrender to him (gold), so also we are a work in progress, dying daily and being redeemed from our old nature (silver). We are being transformed daily, and like the pre-butterfly pupa (cocoon), we are not quite yet a butterfly, but we're no longer a caterpillar. We are being birthed on high, born anew, redeemed, renewed, and made whole in Christ.

Interestingly, the Old Testament conveys in Hebrew the divinity of God (gold) while the New Testament reveals in Greek the redemptive (silver) plan of God in His Son Jesus Christ, who reveals the Father, God. God had planned our honeymoon of eleven days in the Hebrew land and then seven days on a Greek island. It was a precursor of our new life and ministry: Jim's gold ring with Hebrew letters, Shelvy's silver ring with Greek letters, and a honeymoon in the land of the Hebrew and the Greek. It was like the divine and redemptive coming together, the whole Word of God, Old and New Testaments.

Shelvy's View

The morning of our wedding was, like many weddings, a comedy of errors. After still suffering from jet lag, we met before dawn in the lobby of the Nazareth Hotel to find out that we were locked in and the night watchman whom we awoke was lacking the key to let us out. We waited, not so patiently, for him to go to the manager's quarters to retrieve the key. We were to meet John and Paula and others at the church at 7:00 a.m. They were on a tight schedule because they had to drive to Tel Aviv to catch their airplane. We drove the distance as the sun was coming up. It was a new day in our lives, and we sang as we drove along that dusty countryside. The mountain loomed ahead of us, for we could see its great heights from quite a distance. What a glorious place for a couple of eagles to be launched. God sure knows how to do things in style!

Even after arriving at the mountain, we had to make that harrowing drive up to the top by way of all thirty hairpin turns. We kept thinking about Jesus walking all that distance up the mountain with Peter, James, and John. (Read the full account in Matthew 17.) Father Michael was ready for us. He was a monk of the Italian order of Franciscan Fathers. He had set up a special kneeler draped in white, which he was proud to tell us had been used by the Pope several weeks before. In order for the wedding to meet the legal requirements of the Israeli government, Father Michael had to oversee the ceremony and sign the marriage certificate. Jim's pastor at that time, and John Sandford, also officiated at the ceremony. It took three men of God to marry us, so we were thoroughly married. Paula was my (Shelvy's) maid of honor and David, a Messianic Jew we met that day, was Jim's best man. It was just like a fairytale. After we saw John, Paula, and company off, the nuns invited us to their private dining room where they served us a delicious wedding cake that they had baked for us. They presented me with a bouquet of flowers.

We drank in the beauty from the top of the mountain. You could see for miles in every direction. Then we drove down the mountain and to Tiberias, on the Sea of Galilee, where we had a hotel reservation to begin our honeymoon. God not only knows how to plan a wedding but He knows how to plan a honeymoon too! It was glorious! It was "exceedingly abundantly far beyond what we ask or think, according to the power that works in us" (Ephesians 3:20).

⟡

For our twentieth wedding anniversary we returned to the church where we were married and renewed our vows. We retraced the steps of our honeymoon in Greece and Israel. Thank you, God!

Perhaps you would like to pray about your past relationships:

Father God, in the name of Jesus, I come before You, to ask that You heal me of all my past relationships that have been hurtful and disappointing. Forgive my participation in causing these relationships to fail, just as I now choose to forgive those who have wounded me, betrayed me, or abandoned me. Bring to death in me the fear that if I love again, I will be hurt. Give me the grace to trust again and trust You to bring forth the healing I need in order to love, and be loved in a way that is both healthy and brings glory and honor to You. You are the Divine Matchmaker and You know even better than I do what is good and right for me. May we have the privilege of modeling to the world what that heavenly match is like: Christ and His Bride! Amen.

Chapter 3: You Were a Twinkle in God's Eye

We mentioned earlier that God's courtship is far more extensive than romance. Before we can enter into a healthy romance, we need to experience healthy parenting. You may feel that you didn't receive what you needed as an infant or growing child, but regardless of your circumstances, you are God's own love child. His wooing begin before birth and never ends. His ability to reach into your life far exceeds any wound, trauma, or disappointment you may have experienced.

God's great promises for your life still stand, even if you have not yet become aware of their possibility. Your natural and spiritual gifts were given to you way back when God first planned your arrival. Many children grow up just "knowing" things, not knowing how they truly comprehend truth. It takes some observant and discerning adults to nurture these gifts, but their origin is found in the One who created you.

For example, even as a child, I (Shelvy) remember having dreams and then the dream coming true. I used to think in my child-like way, "That's a coincidence!" I gave my life to the Lord when I was ten years old, and I don't remember the church I grew up in teaching about dreams or anything supernatural, but that didn't stop me from experiencing it.

Growing up in the South, going to church was a way of life. My parents enrolled me in the nursery at church when I was just a few days old. We attended most Sunday worship services and Wednesday night prayer meetings. (I didn't understand why they called it a prayer meeting. There was a lot of talking and a little bit of praying.) As the church was not air-conditioned, we kept ourselves cool with fans that were donated by the local funeral home. They were made of paperboard stapled to a wooden handle. One side of the fan proclaimed the name and address of the funeral home and the other side was a picture of Jesus. I loved the scene of Jesus and the little children.

One warm summer day, I was with my mother as she visited a lady friend. While the three of us sat at the dining room table drinking iced tea, I began to feel sorry for the lady. I knew she was going to be in the hospital soon. I don't know how I knew, I just knew. I may have dreamed it but I don't recall. It wasn't anything that they were saying that made me think that. Sure enough, a few days later she was taken to the hospital unexpectedly.

Whenever I would tell my mother of these "coincidences," she wasn't surprised. She would recount to me the circumstances of my birth to help me understand why these things were happening. I was born on September 25th. I loved calling it "Christmas in September." Mother would get that faraway look in her eyes as she remembered the details. She told me that I was born at home with a midwife attending her. She remembers that as I came forth into the world, she heard the church bells ringing. It was Sunday morning at exactly 11 o'clock. The church bells were calling all to come and worship. As a newborn baby, I had a veil (actually, a membrane) over my face. It was believed that this meant the child had a special calling. She and the midwife were convinced of it, especially since I was born as the church bells were ringing.

It was a long time before I knew what a "calling" was. But I loved hearing the story over and over again. I have since come to believe that I was born at the eleventh hour because God has called me to minister in the eleventh hour of the Church.

Jim's Birthing Process

It was probably my (Jim's) mother's prayers that brought me through much of the journey I lived. The first born, I entered the world in troubling times. My mom and dad had met in New York and married at the beginning of the Depression years. I was told that my father had left Norfolk, VA, under a cloud of his family's rejection for his involvement as a "correspondent" in a breach-of-promise trial. A young woman had brought a suit against his friend to enforce the friend's promise to marry her. My father slandered the woman by being a witness (a "correspondent" as it was then called) to her sleeping around (or at least with my father). In court it saved the day for his friend. But I believe this action, joined with his growing alcohol problem, cut off his grace with parents and siblings. You didn't sin and then witness to your sin in a public venue. That scandalized a Southern family's name. He became the "black sheep" of the Wyatt family.

Through my mom's years as a caretaker, she loved to save black sheep. She had worked to complete her studies at the Ontario State College in Ottawa, Canada, and to become a registered nurse. She went from there to the mental wards at the state hospital. I remember her sister, my Aunt May, saying how concerned she was about her in those years. "She was such a little thing going in among those big hulks of men. I worried about her." I believe that she loved the work and knew how to meet their aloneness. Somewhere in her nursing career she turned to private duty for individuals and families. She seemed to love the work and the greater intimacy with the people. It brought her the reward of working with individuals directly until they were well. This case-by-case work was what brought her to New York.

She had a private case in Manhattan and my father was an associate city editor on the night desk of The New York Times when they met and fell in love. They spoke little about those years. I believe my mom held on to some shame of the marriage process and the fact that they needed to marry through a justice of the peace in a civil ceremony. She had been a devout, church-going new convert to Catholicism, but my father had never practiced his Methodist mom's and Presbyterian dad's beliefs. They could not marry in her church since Catholic priests were forbidden to perform "mixed marriages." At a later point in time, the Catholic Church finally officially recognized their marriage. As a result, I wasn't baptized as a Catholic boy until I was five years old. My mother quietly carried shame from those early years. She felt her marriage wasn't real since the church she loved hadn't accepted it. As a boy I knew none of this. The term "mixed marriage" was never spoken of in my growing years. But I believe it resulted in many of my mom's concerns and also her prayers for me.

A Dream...a Remembrance?

I (Jim) would be half asleep when a remembrance would come in a dream-like way. I would be lying on one of our couches late in the afternoon, and I would find myself in a bright green and white murkiness. I could see it all around me. What was strange was that my hands would feel like they were in clay, only it got heavier as I moved or lifted them, and less so if I kept them still. But in the middle of this quiet muffled brightness, I felt vaguely nauseous. I disliked the vision the several times that I had it. What I failed to realize until many years later was that I was remembering my prenatal life. I had been there and lived those moments. Interestingly, I now realize that this particular couch housed the convertible bed my parents slept in during those years. I believe the green-white was the photo-receptor negative of immature prenatal eyes and the heaviness was the walls of the womb. The nauseous feeling was my muffled consciousness —in my hearing and in my spirit—of the turmoil going on in the world outside and in my mom's life and physiology.

I believe my dad felt it was too early in their marriage to take on the responsibility of a child. His drinking problem and job losses created a rage in him that made my mom afraid at times and constantly anxious. When I was nearing adulthood, she confided to me that, occasionally when I was a child, she had worried he might kill me. I have several mysterious scars about which excuses were made. This seems to confirm that statement. That prenatal heaviness was my foreboding about entering a world that was like that. I didn't want to be born. They had to literally come and get me by Caesarian section.

What Does the Unborn Know?

Authors Francis and Judith MacNutt, in their book *Praying For Your Unborn Child*,[10] and John and Paula Sandford, in their book *Healing The Wounded Spirit* refer to the important and eye-opening works of Dr. Thomas Verny.

Dr. Verny is a Canadian-born neurologist and psychiatrist who studied the prenatal development of children. He and many other professional psychologists have found that unborn babies have amazing capabilities. Many of them say that children in the womb can already have memories by the final trimester of the pregnancy, if not sooner than that. There is also proof that unborn babies hear, taste, feel, and learn in the womb and that the experiences in the womb shape a child's attitudes and expectations about himself.[11]

The emotions and thought patterns of the mother have been found to affect the unborn child as well as the father's feelings about his wife and the baby. As a result, if the womb is a friendly and safe place, the baby may be predisposed to good health, happiness, and normal development, if not, the baby may be predisposed to ill health, nervousness, irritability, and arrested development.

---

10. Francis and Judith MacNutt, *Praying for Your Unborn Child*, (New York: Doubleday, 1998).
11. John and Paula Sanford, *Healing The Wounded Spirit*, (Deltona, FL: Victory House, 1985).

After more than 40,000 hours in counseling time, we are convinced that we can be wounded while still in our mothers' wombs. And we also know that our Wonderful Counselor can heal us. Let's look at what the scriptures say:

"For You formed my inward parts; You covered me in my mother's womb. I will praise You, for I am fearfully and wonderfully made; marvelous are Your works, and that my soul knows very well. My frame was not hidden from You, when I was made in secret, and skillfully wrought in the lowest parts of the earth. Your eyes saw my substance, being yet unformed. And in Your book they all were written, the days fashioned for me, when as yet there were none of them" (Psalm 139:13-16).

The most notable of scriptures on prenatal experiences is found in the first chapter of the Gospel of Luke. Mary, a virgin, had an angelic visitation. "And behold, you will conceive in your womb and bring forth a Son and shall call His name Jesus. He will be great, and will be called the Son of the Highest; and the Lord God will give Him the throne of His father David. And He will reign over the house of Jacob forever, and of His kingdom there will be no end" (Luke 1:31-33).

The angel proceeded to tell her, "Elizabeth your relative has also conceived a son in her old age, and this is now the sixth month for her who was called barren" (v. 36).

Mary went to visit Elizabeth. We read in verse 41: "And it happened, when Elizabeth heard the greeting of Mary, that the babe leaped in her womb, and Elizabeth was filled with the Holy Spirit." The unborn child, who would later be called John the Baptist, knew in the womb that they were in the presence of the Son of God! Elizabeth didn't even know that Mary was pregnant. Verse 42 says, "Then she spoke out with a loud voice and said, 'Blessed are you among women, and blessed is the fruit of your womb!'" This is knowledge that was imparted by the Holy Spirit within Elizabeth. She went on to exclaim in verse 43 and 44, "But why is this granted to me, that the mother of my Lord should come to me? For indeed, as soon as the voice of your greeting sounded in my ears, the babe leaped in my womb for joy."

The unborn child, John, experienced joy in the womb. What other emotions does the unborn experience? We would suggest that many have experienced the pain of rejection while in the womb and that has had a profound effect in shaping their lives.

Suicide Attempts: Angela's Story

One such person was a young woman who came for counseling with a history of depression and several suicide attempts. We'll call her "Angela." Angela had lived a hard and painful life. At one of her lowest times, a coworker invited her to come to church. At the church, she was met with welcoming and caring people. This church had a very different atmosphere from the one in her formal religion, where no one ever talked to her and where she seldom felt any comfort for her aching soul. In this new church, she soon was introduced to Someone who cared enough to give His life for her, Jesus Christ. She found that her old forms of comfort—men, alcohol, and partying—felt wrong. As she was learning the Bible, she was convicted that her old way of life displeased the Lord. But without the old ways of self-medicating, the pain became too great to bear.

That is when she came to see me (Shelvy) for the first time. She described to me a life of loneliness from the time she was a child. She was the last child born to her parents. Both of her parents worked outside the home. She said, "We were poor and I felt ashamed of that." When I asked about her father, the answer was, "He was never home, and when he was, we wished he wasn't because he was always drinking."

Next, I began to probe into what I believed would uncover the root of her wounding. I asked about her mother. Her immediate response was, "She was always angry!" Angela had no memories of either parent telling her that they loved her, or of any affection. She always felt that not only was she "not wanted" by her parents, but that her siblings all resented her being born as well. There were fights and name-calling and she, being the youngest, often ended up hurt. She felt vulnerable and worthless because she was not protected or valued. The only person she remembered being kind to her was an aunt, her mother's sister who had never married and had no children. But she saw this aunt infrequently, as she was a flight attendant for one of the major airlines.

Angela described herself as a shy child who just tried to stay out of the way and not draw attention. Attention could mean a slap across the face or more work around the house. She said to me, "I never could figure out what I did wrong that my mother was so angry with me."

As her painful story unfolded, she described her suicide attempts as always being with a sharp object, such as a knife or razor blade. This seemed so ironic to her because she said to me, "I was always afraid of knives or scissors. One of the worst spankings I ever received was because I couldn't bring myself to hand my mother the butcher knife when she told me to. I just couldn't tell her how afraid of it I was."

I knew in my spirit what had happened to this precious girl, but I couldn't tell her. I had to lead her to discovering this information herself. I wrote in her file that I suspected her mother had tried to abort her and probably with a sharp object. She was not the first and I knew she would not be the last that would come with a similar story. I had seen many who unknowingly followed the same pattern of attempted suicide as their mother had followed when she attempted to abort them. For instance, if the mother had tried pills, very often that was what the person used in attempting to end their own life.

I suggested that Angela contact her aunt and try to find out all she could about the circumstances of her conception and of her months in the womb. She returned with a story that confirmed my suspicions. In her own words, "My aunt said my mother was at her wits' end with too many children, too little money, and no help from my father. The last thing she needed was another mouth to feed and another child to be responsible for. She tried to abort me using a coat hanger! My mother called my aunt because she couldn't stop the bleeding and was really scared. She got a bad infection but I survived the attempted abortion."

This explained a lot to me. I held Angela in my arms as she cried and we prayed to forgive her mother. She also asked the Lord to forgive her for trying to take her own life.

As you have read this story, perhaps you have identified with Angela, knowing the pain of rejection and the deep feelings of abandonment from never bonding with her mother while being carried in the womb. Angela needs to choose life again and again until the message is received in her heart that God loves her, that she was not a mistake or accident. Would you pray with me?

Father God, in the name of Jesus, I come before You confessing that I have despaired of life. Believing that I was not wanted, I have failed to embrace life. I renounce the lie that says, "I'm a mistake, I'm not chosen, I'm not loved, I'm not even worthy of being loved!" I choose this day to believe that God is the giver of all life and that I am His own "love-child," conceived in His heart and mind before I was ever implanted in my mother's womb. I thank You, Lord that You ordained my gender and I am exactly what You wanted me to be. I choose to embrace the sexuality You chose for me. I forgive my parents for wanting a different sex for me. You don't make mistakes and You don't make junk. I am "fearfully and wonderfully made!" Bring to death in me all the lies I have believed about myself, and resurrect in me new life, a life that will bring honor and glory to You as I fulfill my destiny for my life! Amen.

If you identified more with Angela's mother and did have an abortion, pray with me:

Father God, I come to You in sackcloth and ashes, overcome with a new understanding of what I have done. Oh, Lord, I took my child's life to save myself from difficulty, inconvenience, embarrassment or responsibility. I heartlessly and selfishly ended a precious life, one You created and gave to me and to this world. To cover the pain and guilt of my act I hardened my heart and have lived in denial and secrecy. Every part of my life has been stained by this sin, every relationship damaged. The pain I refused to feel is killing me in return. But Father, You have pursued me with Your truth and Your unconditional love. And so I come to You to ask Your forgiveness for what I have done. My sin seems unforgivable to me, yet I know You want nothing more than to set me free from the bondage of my act, to turn my hardened, unloving heart into a soft and compassionate heart of flesh. Only You in Your divine mercy can offer such forgiveness. Forgive me, O Lord, and be with me and comfort me as I now grieve the great loss of my child. In Jesus' Name, Amen.[12]

And now, I would like to offer a prayer for each woman reading this that has had a miscarriage, an abortion, a stillborn or death of a baby while still in the womb.

Father God, Giver of life, come with the cleansing waters of Your Holy Spirit and cleanse every womb that has been a tomb. Release the balm of Gilead for healing of the memories within this womb and throughout this woman. Heal the memories of all trauma and shock that interrupted the pregnancy that was filled with new life. Receive unto Yourself the precious life that was terminated for whatever

---

12. A Prayer of Grieving For An Abortion, Elijah House, Basic II School For Prayer Ministry.

reason. Let this womb now become a safe place for new life. I thank You, Lord that You make all things new! In Jesus' name, Amen.

Perhaps as you have read Angela's story, you are reminded that you did not want to be pregnant with one of your children. Perhaps you weren't married and felt the shame of that. Perhaps you had to get married because of that pregnancy and you're not sure your husband would have married you otherwise. While you did not abort your child, neither did you rejoice over it or embrace it as a precious gift from God.

Were you hoping and even praying for your child to be a different gender than what it was? Are you still angry with God because He didn't give you what you wanted? Have you blamed God because you have a "special needs" child? Have you entertained thoughts like, *I don't deserve this*, or *is God punishing me for some sin I've committed*?

Pray with me:

Father God, in the name of Jesus, I come before you confessing that I am guilty of trying to play God. You are the giver of life. You see the end from the beginning and You alone know Your purposes for each life. You know the perfect time for a life to come forth. Forgive me for being so shortsighted that I have judged You as not knowing what You are doing. Forgive me of my sins concerning all that has come to mind and that which I don't even remember. I thank You, Lord, that You are my Redeemer and You are bigger than my mistakes and sins. Thank You for the gift of life, my life and the lives of my children. Amen.

God is the Creator of time, therefore He is not confined by it as we are. While we must live in time, Jesus does not. Through prayer, we can invite God to go back in time to pour healing into whatever painful memories are part of our personal history. We can be set free from the bondages of a painful past, even if that past dates back to our time in the womb.

Grace Comes Out of Depression:

I (Shelvy) am reminded of a sixteen-year-old girl who was brought to me by her mother. It was January and school was back in session after the winter break for the holidays. But Grace had not gone back to school with her classmates. She was deeply depressed, slept all day, wouldn't take phone calls from friends, stayed in her room, and some days she refused to get dressed. This had been going on ever since Christmas. At first, Grace's mother thought she was sick. But trips to the doctor and blood tests found nothing wrong, at least not with her body. Questioning Grace proved fruitless. She didn't know why she was depressed, she just was. She didn't want to think about her life, so she was trying to sleep it away.

I saw on Grace's counseling questionnaire that her birthday was in July, and I began to suspect that maybe this depression had something to do with her conception and her mother's response to being pregnant with her. This would be about the time of the year when her mother would find out that she was pregnant. I prayed silently that the Holy Spirit would reveal what we needed to know.

Her mother helped with the family history. Grace's father was a Naval officer, her mother sold real estate. There were three siblings, all older and out of the home. Then the story began to take shape. When the youngest of the three was thirteen years old, Grace's mother found out she was pregnant. It was the middle of December when the pregnancy test came back positive. In her own words, the mother said, "I just wouldn't let myself think about it. I had too much to do in preparation for Christmas. And I was studying for my real estate license exam." I asked how she felt about having a fourth child. Her reply was, "I really thought it was a mistake, the positive pregnancy test...I mean. I thought I was

66

probably going through early menopause. So I didn't even say anything to my husband. I would just get through the real estate exam and the holidays."

Then she said something that made me think I was on the right track of playing detective, with the Holy Spirit's leading. It seemed I had struck a nerve. Grace's mother said, "Why are we talking about me? We're here for Grace. She's the one who needs help!" She proceeded to tell me that this was the second year that this had happened to Grace. "Last year, after Christmas, she got sick, and I thought it was the flu. She stayed in bed and withdrew from everyone. She just didn't want to go back to school. Now I'm thinking maybe it wasn't the flu after all but depression instead. But after awhile she snapped out of it and went back to school."

I tried to lay a foundation of belief that the "little one" in the womb can pick up on the emotions in the mother. Was it possible that as the pregnancy with Grace became a reality that her mother became depressed? Grace's mother began to cry and say, "We love Grace and we're glad God blessed us with her. But you're right. I was upset and depressed that, at my age, I was pregnant again." I remember now that, after Christmas was over, all I wanted to do was go back to bed after getting my husband off to work and the children off to school. If I could sleep, I wouldn't have to think about it. But after awhile, I accepted the fact that we were going to have a baby. My husband was actually excited about it. And truth be known, Grace has been a joy and delight, keeping us young. I think we have enjoyed her more because we were more mature parents this time around.

Grace had a lot of questions for her mother but had no problem forgiving her. We prayed, or I should say, I prayed, and they cried. The following year, during the winter school break, Grace came to see me. She wanted me to know she was fine, no depression. Even, the following year, which was her first year in college, she sent me a note saying the same thing: "No depression." God is so good! His ways are beyond our understanding. So we act in faith, believing He is Who He says He is and trusting that He will work all things together for our good.

Donna Laughs Last

For many, the destructive circumstances of their births continue to be reinforced through their early lives. I remember a young woman—we'll call her Donna—who was in her thirties when we met her at a retreat where we were speakers. We liked her. She was gentle and open to us and began seeing Shelvy for personal counseling. I (Jim) would sometimes join them in her sessions to tell her a funny story or joke I had just heard. At the time she always seemed self-conscious and slightly depressed. I felt the need to lift her spirits and affirm her. We noticed, however, that whenever I talked to her she would keep looking at Shelvy, as if for guidance in how to react. She was afraid to let go and react or laugh on her own. It was painful to see but I kept encouraging her with a cheerful story or a gentle hug. The Lord seems to guide me as to when a person needs a father's affirmation.

One time she mentioned that her father always seemed to reject her and call her "Dummy" or "Stupid," never by her real name. Shelvy knew this was a clue to her hurting. She revealed that because of her lack of confidence, she always signed on with temporary job agencies for work. She felt that if she stayed in one place too long they would discover, to her shame, that she was dumb or stupid.

Shelvy instructed Donna to seek out an older relative to question on the circumstances surrounding her conception, birth, and her mother's pregnancy. When she did quiz an older sister, she was told "Mom and dad were separated before you were born and there was another man." When Donna then asked her mother, she told her in tears about her real father. It seems that her mother and "father" had separated for a year and a half. Another man had befriended her mom during that time. But her parents got back together again to work things out only to discover her mom was pregnant. It's no wonder her "father" chose to act as he did. He refused to forgive the mother and the child for the pregnancy. Donna was a constant reminder of her mother's unfaithfulness to him.

Donna remembered her true (birth) father as a "friend of the family." He was always around during her childhood. He'd talk to her through the schoolyard fence, asking her how she was doing. He attended her first Communion, confirmation, school plays, graduation, and other events. He always stood in the background.

Upon hearing these revelations, she decided to contact him and invite him out for coffee. She bravely met him with much trepidation as to how he might respond. When she related her new-found truths to him, he opened up to her in tears. He told her that he had always loved her mother and her. "I never married because she was the only one. I still love her." He had longed to be a part of her life, but her mother had instructed him to stay away so she could work out her marriage for the sake of the four children. Now at last Donna and her birth father began to develop their father/daughter relationship. It is still growing.

Donna was able to forgive her step-father, birth-mother and birth-father. She also started letting go of the old pictures of herself in her mind's eye. I knew she was on her way when one day she proudly stated, "I told a joke yesterday."

"Oh! Let me hear it,"

"I was in the dentist's chair and the dentist was behind me, humming and singing as he rummaged through his instrument drawers. I turned toward him and said, 'It's too bad about your parents spending all that money.'

'What money?' he said.

69

I said, 'You know…for your singing lessons.' He laughed." And she and I laughed together. She was on her way to the healing of long-held hurts and knowing that she really was smart and lovable.

What's in a Name?

Many years ago, we ministered to a couple, distraught over their first-born son. He was always getting into trouble and had been doing so since he was a baby. They were at the end of their rope. They had corrected, punished, lectured, bribed, and done everything else suggested. But nothing seemed to work. Well-meaning friends and relatives even said maybe he was "bad seed." The behavioral problems followed him into school, and his teachers felt he was not learning according to his potential. He was tested for learning disabilities but none were found.

After praying and asking for the Holy Spirit's guidance, we began to play detective. Both parents were cooperative in answering our questions: "Yes, we were married when our son was conceived, and yes we were excited and wanted a child at that time and especially a boy to carry on the family name." The boy was named after his father. The mother had a healthy pregnancy and delivery. There had been no accidents or illnesses that may have traumatized the boy. He had not manifested any symptoms of being abused in any way. The mother was a stay-at-home mom so the boy wasn't being neglected or mistreated in any way.

Just when it appeared we were running into a dead end, we asked the father, whom the boy was named after, "What do you call him: 'William,' 'Bill,' 'Billy'?" Then we hit "pay dirt." The grandfather (father's father) had lived with them since the boy was born and immediately started calling him "Rebel." The name stuck and throughout his ten years of life, their first-born son was called "Rebel" by one and all. It almost seemed to be too simple. Was the boy merely living up to his name? Was his behavior now defining who he was? Both parents stared at us with that "No, it couldn't be" look on their faces. We gave them biblical illustrations like Abigail's husband, Nabal, whose name means "fool" and that he lived up to his name (as recorded in 1 Samuel 25), The more they thought about it, they were willing to act on this revelation. They offered a prayer of repentance for allowing their son to be called "Rebel" all those years. They had participated in the problem and now they wanted to be a part of the solution. This is what they did:

They instructed their son that he was not to be called "Rebel" again and they did not want him to respond to being called that name, but rather, he was to correct it by stating that his name is "William." They explained that *William* means "protector" and expressed what a noble spirit he'd been given. They called a family meeting and instructed their younger children and the boy's grandfather that William was no longer to be called by the nickname "Rebel." They sent a letter to his teacher, school bus driver, boy's club leader, baseball coach, Sunday school teacher, and everyone else they could think of who was in their son's life. They informed his friends, one by one as they came to visit. They exerted every effort and were diligent in doing all they could do.

Both mother and father looked for every opportunity to praise new and better behavior. They also affirmed and blessed every effort the boy made to change. While still holding him accountable for his behavior, they consistently demonstrated unconditional love. Little by little, these parents saw that their own attitudes toward their son were changing because they had given God permission to bring to death their negative expectations of him.

The results were amazing! Within one school year, this "failing student" became an above-average "B" student. The rebellious behavior and attitudes were overcome by the transforming power of love.

God is interested in the names we are called. He gave us dominion to call things into His blessings and it's no small thing for us to do so in His eyes. Throughout biblical history people were named in alignment with God's purposes for their lives. Jesus is the prime example because the name *Jesus* means "God is my salvation" and He is the only One to have perfectly fulfilled His name.

The Baby Who Refused to be Born

A young couple sat before us, parents of a one-year-old son. The wife was in discomfort as she shifted her position on the sofa, trying to find a way to sit that would give her some relief. She was nine months pregnant, or I should say, nine months plus. Their first child had come two weeks before term. But she was overdue and anxious to give birth to this child who they referred to as Ruth Ann. They had not planned a second child so soon after the first one. But they had accepted this pregnancy with joy, believing that God would provide. From the beginning of the pregnancy, the wife believed God told her that they were going to have a girl, so they named the baby Ruth Ann and called the baby by that name for most of the nine months. The husband faithfully prayed over the baby and blessed the baby as it was growing and developing in his wife's womb.

We suggested to them that possibly it wasn't Ruth Ann but rather a second son who was growing in the womb. And just maybe he hesitated to come forth because he knew they would be disappointed. The young wife insisted, "No, I know God told me that I am having a girl."

Then the husband asked us, "But what if you are right, what could we do about it now?"

Our reply was, "First, ask God's forgiveness for the possible presumption of the gender of the child and calling the baby Ruth Ann for nine months. Second, pray over the baby and speak directly to it and tell your baby that you want it, you love it, and ask forgiveness for calling it by a girl's name. Tell the baby that you want it, no matter if it's a girl or a boy. Welcome the baby as

72

a perfect addition to your family. The baby won't understand your words but we believe it will know in its heart what you are saying."

They followed our counsel that night, praying and talking to the baby just before going to bed. Two hours later, the young wife woke up in labor and before morning, their second son was born! We told the parents to continue to pray healing for their baby boy who had been addressed as a little girl for all those many months.

No matter what the circumstances of our conception, the time we spend in the womb, or our delivery experience, each of us began with Him. In Genesis 15, we read of Abram talking with God about Abram's lack of offspring. "Then He brought him outside and said, 'Look now toward heaven and count the stars if you are able to number them.' And He said to him, 'So shall your descendants be.'" Every time Abram saw the stars twinkle in the heavens at night, he was reminded of God's promise to him.

We would suggest that when you look into the heavens and see the stars twinkle, remember, God is the Life-Giver. And you were conceived in His heart and mind before you were ever implanted in your mother's womb. The Father, Son, and Holy Spirit danced over you. Long before you were a twinkle in your earthly father's eye, you were a twinkle in God's eye! He loves you with an everlasting love and nothing that you can do will ever make Him stop loving you. His love for us has the power to transform our lives forever!

Chapter 4: Wonderful Counselor, Mighty Healer

She sat across from me (Shelvy) for the first time, and I could see shame and pain all over her. There was nothing to see with the naked eye, but I could see with my mind's eye. She was attractive but you couldn't convince her of that. She was intelligent and successful by all the standards of the world of commerce. But I knew she didn't come for a counseling session thinking she was successful. She was hurting, and I could read the hidden messages of her heart: *If you knew me as I really am, you wouldn't like me. If you knew what I've done, you'd blame me just as I've blamed myself! How can I possibly tell you, and will it do any good? Will it make some of the pain and shame go away?*

After praying my all-time favorite prayer, *Help, Lord! Come, Holy Spirit, Come!* I listened to the familiar words, "I've never told anyone this before…"

I could write the script, just change the characters. Who is it this time—father, brother, uncle, grandfather, neighbor, or close family friend? Rarely is it a stranger, although that happens sometimes. Most of the time it is someone the child trusted who victimized them. They are robbed of their innocence and go away feeling that they are bad and dirty.

All little children live by an unwritten code that says, *If something bad happens to me, it's because I'm bad, I'm unworthy, I'm unlovable.* In their innocence they believe "the big people do

75

everything right and therefore if anything goes wrong it must be my fault." The unfounded anger and accusations against the child only serve to reinforce their belief further. As the child grows and leaves childhood behind, these false messages are still written on the heart. Because we live out of our heart—"As a man thinks in his heart so is he" (Proverbs 23:7), they now have a negative expectation that they will be abused again and somehow it will be their own fault.

I (Shelvy) have had women say to me, "I feel like I'm wearing a sign that says, 'Abuse Me!' I always end up with those who will hurt me and take advantage of me." But Jesus came to take all our guilt and shame to death on the cross.

If this sounds like you (the reader) or someone you know, be encouraged because one of the ways God redeems the pain of our past is to heal us and then use us in His healing of others.

Sexual Abuse

When I (Shelvy) was a young girl, my father's business partner touched me inappropriately. They had built a new building for their business. I don't know why I was in that empty room alone with this man but he came up behind me and his touch was unexpected and unwanted. It was such a violation of my childhood innocence that I immediately reached out to feel the texture of the plastered wall. I had to escape the reality of the moment. As is the case with most children, I did not tell anyone. I felt I was bad and afraid I'd get in trouble.

I completely suppressed the memory for more than twenty years. It was only after I had gone through some inner healing that I had enough strength to experience the remembered pain and shame and allow the memory to come up to my conscious mind. I had the symptoms of someone who had been abused. I had struggled with my weight all my life. When the bad feelings would

76

come, food was a major distraction and comfort. *If I hide myself in a blanket of fat, no one will find me attractive and I'll be safe.*

Another symptom was that I didn't trust men. I didn't understand this while growing up because my father was a very gentle and peaceful man and had never been abusive in any way. One day, when I was a young woman, I was praying about my father's death when I was a teenager. I felt angry toward him, although I knew it wasn't his fault that he had cancer and died. But what rose up in me was the scene of my childhood victimization, and with it, the cry of a young child: *Where was my father? Why didn't he know what kind of man his partner was? Why didn't he protect me?*

Although my father had no knowledge of what happened to me, he was appointed by God to protect his children, as are all fathers. I chose to forgive him for not being there for me, as my protector. I forgave the man who had violated my innocence. And I forgave myself for believing the lies, that somehow I had caused this awful thing to happen, that I was bad, unlovable, and unworthy. I asked the Lord to write a new message on my heart about myself and also about men.

Jeremiah 17:1 says, "The sin of Judah is written with a pen of iron; with the point of a diamond it is engraved on the tablet of their heart." Just as the people of Judah had such a hard heart that only a pen of iron with a diamond tip could write a message on their hearts, such was the condition of my heart. I had hardened my heart so I was numb to the pain. I didn't cry but was very sad and melancholy. Not only did I block out the bad but also the good. I was robbed of the joy of life. I am so very thankful for God's patience to work with me and heal me of this childhood hurt.

Perhaps you can identify with what I have shared from my childhood experience. And perhaps you are thinking, *But it only happened once.* It only happened once for me, but I lived in fear that it would happen again. Such is the case with many children.

Would you pray with me?

Father God, in the name of Jesus, I come before you, bringing my pain and my anger. Where were You? Why didn't You protect me? Why did You allow this awful thing to happen to me? Can I ever trust You or anyone again? Can You really heal me and make me whole?

I choose this day to believe that You are Who You say You are in Your Word, the Holy Scriptures. I ask that You would come to heal my broken heart and my tormented mind. Heal the memories within me of what happened in my childhood; the images in my mind, the smells and sounds, the feelings that rise up in me, even the memories within my body and my sexuality. Sever my spirit from the spirit of my victimizer. Place me under the giant waterfall of the cleansing waters of Your Holy Spirit. Wash away all the shame and blame I have internalized.

I choose to forgive the one that wounded me and violated my childhood innocence. I place that person in Your hands because Your Word says, 'Vengeance is Mine, I will repay,' says the Lord. You do what You will. I give up all thoughts of revenge and bitterness. I want to be free of any further power this person has over me.

I choose to forgive myself for every way I blamed myself: For believing I am responsible because I was in the wrong place at the wrong time. For believing that I could have caused this awful thing to happen to me by some word or action on my part. For believing that I didn't deserve to be protected, and for believing that I was bad and unworthy. Bring to death in me the lies I have believed because of that childhood hurt, the sinful habits and self-destructive practices, the false forms of comfort and the guilt for perhaps enjoying the attention, or for the feelings as my body responded the way it was designed to. Resurrect in me hope that the future will be better than the past, a healthy love and respect for myself, and wisdom to set boundaries that are appropriate. Grant me a mind renewed in truth and love for others and for myself.

I choose to forgive You, Father God, for all the ways I've blamed You. I know You are not guilty of any wrongdoing, but I need to release these offences against You that I have held in my childhood heart. Thank You for hearing my prayer. Amen.

Sexual-Identity Confusion

Just as we can be confused about what our purpose is in life, we are often confused about our own identity as male or female. If a son is rejected by his father, either by overt abuse or by covert neglect, then he has not been loved to life and he senses this as his own inferiority. With his own nature or "maleness" being continually denied, he may seek to find those parts of his "being-ness" elsewhere, or in another. We are not talking here of simple masculine traits or qualities, such as independence or problem-solving skills. Although men typically have these in greater abundance, women can have them, too. Just as men can have female qualities, but more often in lesser capacity. What we are speaking of is a more specific need to receive male sexual identity. Sexual abuse to a boy, that is, being sexually awakened by another male, can create sexual identity confusion.

Same-sex attraction occurs when that son might be overly attracted to males, seeing in them what he wishes for, but no longer believes he has the ability in himself to be what he desires. His maleness has been so unloved or denied in himself that he now erroneously believes it can only be obtained by taking it from another male.

God sees it as a wounding that only He can heal. We've seen Him heal and transform many and lead them out of that lifestyle and into a new way of life.

Sometimes a daughter sees something in the modeling of the mother that causes her to say, "If that's what it means to be a woman, no thanks!" Especially when she sees the mother being a "doormat" for the man, or if the mother is sickly and weak, or has a really rough life, filled with responsibilities and hardship. If the life of her mother was one of abuse, it conveyed the message that it is not safe to be female.

The daughter's response may be to quench her femaleness and become more masculine in her thinking and demeanor. Down deep, she concludes that it is not safe or desirable to be female. There are usually many inner vows and judgments that will have to be dealt with in order for the daughter to be set free to live the life that God ordained for her.

Jamie's Story

Many years ago, I (Shelvy) ministered to a woman who had chosen, out of her woundedness, to live in a same-sex relationship. She lived with another woman who was divorced and had children by an abusive husband. It took awhile for her to trust me. She was afraid that I would judge and condemn her, as many had in the past. It wasn't until her pain and desperation led her to attempt suicide that she became serious about getting some help.

Through many tears and much pain, her story came out. She was an unwanted child, born to parents more than forty years of age and both alcoholics. She was only a few weeks old, when the neighbor in the next apartment called the mother's sister, complaining that the baby had been crying for hours and no one would come to the door. Upon entering the apartment, they found the baby had been left alone, had a dirty diaper and was hungry. It was days before they heard from the parents. Not wanting to get her sister in trouble with the law, this older sister took the baby home with her. The woman I was ministering to said, "My aunt did the best she could, but she was in her fifties and resented having to be bothered with a child at her age. Her husband, my uncle, was not kind but abusive. Not only did he use me sexually as I got older, but he made money by passing me around to his friends. I ran away as a young teenager and made my own way as best I could.

"I met a woman at work who treated me with kindness and would often invite me to her house for a meal with her and her children. After a while, I moved in. She took me to her Pentecostal church where I became a Christian. Soon she and I became lovers. At first, those were the happy years in my life. I helped with her children and became like the father they never had. We would play ball, go fishing—all the things I never got to do growing up. It wasn't long before I decided God had made a mistake, I really was a man in a woman's body. That belief became confirmed to me when I stopped having my monthly menstrual periods. After a few months, I went to the doctor. He had no explanation for why I had ceased my menses. The happiness seemed short-lived; I was miserable inside. I was torn between wanting to go on as a Christian and continuing to live with someone who was safe and, I felt, loved me. It didn't seem I could have both."

Thus, she and I (Shelvy) began many hours of prayer, instruction in the Bible and renouncing inner vows, bitter root judgments and expectancies. I led her in a prayer of forgiveness and healing. I was seated across from her and had my eyes closed as we prayed. In my mind's eye, I saw into her abdomen. It was a shocking sight, what looked like two black and piercing eyes looked out at me. It was like a creature with many tentacles. The tentacles were wrapped around her Fallopian tubes. It was brownish-red, like old dried blood.

Without telling her what I was seeing, I began to pray the scriptures, taking authority over that which was not of Him and commanded in Jesus' name that she be loosed. I saw a two-edged sword enter into her abdomen as I spoke, and, as it was drawn out, the creature followed.

Then I opened my eyes because I heard her drop to the floor on all fours and say, "Thank you, Jesus. Thank you, Jesus, for setting me free." She was crying tears of joy. Later, I told her what I saw.

This all happened on a Saturday. Sunday morning when she woke up, she found that she had started her monthly menstrual period. What was so unusual about this is she had not had her menses in several years and the doctor had been unable to find out why. So on Monday morning, she went to her doctor and told him what happened on Saturday. He confirmed that she had been healed, writing her a letter saying that she had been healed by the power of prayer to the Lord Jesus Christ. He was a Christian and knew that a miracle had taken place. What a mighty God we serve! There is nothing too difficult for Him. He is still in the miracle healing business!

Our identity is not to be found in another but has been put within us by God. It is best brought forth through the eyes of a loving father. Only our heavenly Father can redeem that which was denied or not "called forth" (confirmed) by an earthly father, for He is a "father to the fatherless" (Psalm 10:14; 68:5; 146:9). The Hebrew word *'ab* for "father"[13] is supposed to be one of the first words a baby can speak. (It would be wonderful if it were our last, too!)

Great Expectations

I believe that the first wound against my (Shelvy's) sexuality occurred when I was still being formed in my mother's womb. It was an inconvenient time for my parents to be having a second

---

13. *Strong's Exhaustive Concordance*, s.v., H2, " 'ab."

child. They had a baby girl who was just a little over a year old when they learned I was on the way.

Although they never said this to me, I believe they wanted me to be a boy. And that is perfectly understandable as they had already made one of the "other kind." While it is natural for parents to have a preference as to the sex of their unborn child, that can be quite wounding, even creating sexual-identity confusion. Out of that sexual-identity confusion can come same-sex attraction. The child's logic goes like this: If I am a female, and my parents didn't want a girl, they didn't want me. The result is rejection of the child's identity. After all, it is the boy who carries on the family name. I knew in my spirit that I was the "wrong kind" and a disappointment. I tried to make up for the fact that my father never got a son. I would help him in all the ways a boy would, like doing yard work, cutting wood, car-washing, and even repairs. I wanted his approval.

I believe this was the beginning of rejection in my life. The "Oh, no!" upon finding out that a second child had been conceived and then, at birth, the "Another girl." This rejection was specifically against my sexuality as a female. This is not to say that my parents didn't love me, I know they did. They demonstrated their love every day by the sacrifices they made, large and small.

Parents' preference for a particular sex for their unborn child can produce sexual-identity confusion. We know of a mother who wanted a girl after giving birth to four boys so she dressed her new baby boy in girl's clothes for the first two years of his life. It's easy to see why this would cause confusion for the child.

Another cause can be the absence of the same-sex parent from the life of the child; he or she has only the opposite-sex parent with whom to identify. They are missing the one God had ordained to bless the child in his or her sexuality and call forth to life in the fullness of his or her uniqueness. Each child needs to be separated from their mother, as surely as the umbilical cord must be cut.

Sometimes when a boy lives with a harsh or cruel father and watches his abusiveness, the son decides that if his father is defining what it means to be a male, then "No, thank you!" The boy rejects the father's model. From there on, he may be seeking his masculinity in another male. In like manner, when a mother models to her daughter a life that says, "I am a victim, I'm a doormat, I'm sickly, and therefore it is not safe or good to be female," the girl says, "No, thank you!" In rejecting her mother's "femaleness," she rejects her own femaleness. She may then try to seek her femaleness in an inappropriate relationship with other females who she admires and wants to be like, all the while denying her own God-given femininity. Parents are the first authority figures in the life of the child, so whatever they do or say has great power in it for that child.

If you suspect that your parents may have wanted you to be one of the "other kind" and not the sex that you are, pray with me:

Father God, in the name of Jesus, I choose to forgive my parents for wanting me to be different from what and who I am. I know that I am exactly the sex you wanted me to be. Heal the wounds against my sexuality and pour Your wholeness into me. Let me glory in my sexuality. Bring to death in me the confusion concerning my sexuality. I know You are not the author of confusion. I confess that I have been seeking my identity in wrongful relationships. Take the mighty sword of Your Spirit and sever my spirit from each person I have attached myself to in an unlawful and unholy way. Cleanse my spirit and my sexuality from all defilement caused by these relationships.

Forgive me for the judgments I have made against my parents. I desire to be obedient to Your Word by honoring my parents because they gave me life. I forgive them for not modeling to me a healthy and holy model of masculinity and femininity.

Father God, come and "re-parent" me. Teach me how to live true to who You made me to be, male or female. Teach me how to relate in a healthy and holy way to the opposite sex as well as the same sex. Bring to death in me those structures of thinking, habits, and practices that cause me to sin. Resurrect in me new life and hope for a better tomorrow. Thank You for Your faithfulness to answer this prayer. Amen.

Adoption and Rejection

We are aware that many who are reading this may have been adopted. You may have experienced rejection in the womb because your mother knew you would be given up through adoption. Perhaps your father never even knew you had been conceived. When your birth parents came together, not only was a new life begun, there was a promise born in your spirit that they would love you and care for you. We are talking about an inner knowing, that part of us that understands what we know even though we don't comprehend. We have had people who were adopted as babies tell us they always felt something was wrong, that they were wrong, they just didn't belong even though they were raised in loving homes. That promise was broken for whatever reason. It may have been a loving sacrifice to give you up for adoption. It may have been because your mother died. You may not know all, or any of the reasons why. But we know there was a tearing in the fabric of your being and God wants to mend it with His healing power.

Listen to what the Lord says: "When my father and my mother forsake me, then the Lord will take care of me" (Psalm 27:10). "A father of the fatherless, a defender of widows, is God in His holy habitation. God sets the solitary in families" (Psalm 68:5-6). God promises, "I will never leave you nor forsake you" (Hebrews 13:5).

If you have felt rejected by your parents, pray with me:

Prayer for Rejection:

Father God, I come to You, broken and rejected, forsaken by those who promised to love and care for me. Pour Your healing power into me and make me whole. Cause me to know in my innermost being that I am wanted, chosen, and loved. I choose to believe Your Word that You will never forsake me. Renew my mind with those truths that will transform me by Your love. Bring to death in me those ways of thinking that cause me to reject myself and sometimes, even harm myself. Forgive me for the many times I have rejected others before they could reject me. I don't want to do that anymore. Root and ground me in the reality of Your love. Let me know that acceptance that anchors my soul when the storms of life come. Thank You for Your faithfulness to continue answering this prayer, even when my mind has grown so old that I don't remember praying this day. May You be glorified in and through my life. Amen.

Adoptive Parents Did It Right

We have good friends who had prayed and waited for nine long years. They longed for a precious child to adopt. Believing that it must not be in God's plan for them, they surrendered their dream and cried and grieved their loss. The next day, the Lord resurrected their dream. They received a call from the adoption agency that a baby girl had just been born and they were to come to the hospital the next morning. From the first moment they laid eyes on her, they knew she was worth the long wait. She was both beautiful and healthy! After bringing her home, they didn't just pray over her one time, but many times. They knew to pray for healing of the wound of rejection and any lack of bonding with the birth mother. They asked the

Lord to go back to her conception and bathe the whole nine months of her formation in the womb with the healing power of His love. They spoke God's words of affirmation to her spirit, that she was His own love child, conceived in His heart and mind before she was ever implanted in her mother's womb.

We have had the privilege to know and love this child from the time she was two days old. She is exceptional! She is secure in the knowledge that she is loved. She gave her heart to Jesus when she was only five years old. One of her favorite play activities was to play "church." She would line up her dolls and stuffed animals and preach to them.

These adoptive parents did it right from the beginning. The fruit of their obedience "to train up their child in the ways of the Lord" can be seen in her. Not only does she know that she is loved but she also loves much. What a joy she is to all who know her. We believe she is destined for greatness.

"Now to Him who is able to do exceedingly abundantly above all that we ask or think" (Ephesians 3:20).

Dyslexia

I (Shelvy) never felt good about myself growing up. Never thought I was smart, never thought I was intelligent. Because I saw some numbers and letters backward, I thought I was dumb. I worked very hard to make sure no one ever knew my shameful secret. It wasn't until I was out of high school that I learned about dyslexia. What I read in that textbook about learning disabilities described me! I now knew there was a name for it. I have since come to believe that I didn't want to be born; in my spirit I knew I would be a disappointment to my parents. John Sandford, my spiritual father, explained to me that my spirit turned around to flee back into the womb and my mental capacities were turned around with it.

John and Paula Sandford wrote an excellent book, *Healing The Wounded Spirit*,[14] which covers this subject. After reading the book, I prayed and asked the Lord to forgive me for not wanting to be born. I needed to choose life! I also asked the Lord to make my spirit right within me; I no longer have dyslexia. Maybe this sounds too simple to be true but all I can say is, "This is what happened to me."

Turned Around

One mother tells me the story of her son who, in kindergarten and first grade, was struggling in school. He was a sweet child, but he had a hard time paying attention and was often writing his alphabet letters backward. He also slept so deeply it was hard to wake him up each day. His teachers understood that some of his learning issues might have been emotionally based (the boy's father had been abusive and had recently left the family.) Nonetheless, they were alert to the possibility that he might have a mild disability. His mother prayed that the Lord would give her His wisdom as to how to help her son.

One day soon after she'd prayed, she was playing a cassette tape in her car—a collection of songs the family was practicing for a mission trip. Much to her surprise, instead of songs, the voices of John and Paula Sandford came through the car speakers. *What?* She thought, puzzled; she re-checked the tape to see if she had the right one. She did; the songs were recorded over an old cassette, on the other side. Her interest peaked, she listened to what the Sandfords had to say.

"We had our son tested, and they told us he was either an idiot or a genius," they said. Apparently, the Sandford's son had

---

14. John and Paula Sanford, *Healing The Wounded Spirit*, (Deltona, FL: Victory House, 1985).

experienced a few school struggles of his own! Riveted to learn more, this mother listened closely. The Sandfords shared how the Lord revealed a connection to them between their son's birth experience and his learning symptoms. He'd been facing backward in the womb with the umbilical cord wrapped around his neck at first; the birth had been risky. The Lord directed them to pray that he would "choose life" and face forward. His spirit was evidently facing "backward" within him, resulting in backward letters and so on. When they prayed in this way, the Sandford's son began to turn around indeed. His learning issues cleared up dramatically.

Armed with this timely insight, this young mother prayed for her son. She also talked with him directly. "I'm wondering if, before you were born, part of you didn't want to come out because you knew it would be hard?" she said.

Immediately he dissolved in tears. "Yeeah!" he cried. It was as though he was relieved to have these deeper feelings recognized.

"I think I learned about something we can pray that will help that part of you feel better, and maybe also help with school work," she told him. After praying for God to heal the hurts he'd sustained during the years of abuse, she prayed for her son's spirit to choose life and face forward. "Can you say that? 'I choose life?'" she asked him.

He said it after her: "I choose life." The very next morning, he was much easier to wake up. And in a matter of days, this little boy's letters began to turn around and face forward too. All because of a mother's prayers and the Lord's mysterious provision of the "wrong" side of the cassette!

Double Rejection, Double Redemption

My good friend (I'll call her Helen) has suffered one of the worst cases of dyslexia I have ever seen. Her young parents had been married just a short time when she was conceived. They were delighted and eagerly awaited the arrival of their baby. But when time for the delivery came something went wrong—very wrong. All eyes were drawn away from the newborn because the young mother was fighting for her life. A fight she lost, because Helen's mother died just hours after her birth. Her grief-stricken father would have nothing to do with her. He deposited her with his elderly parents and left to join the Army. Her grandparents did the best they could, but they resented being saddled with a newborn. This was not the way they had planned to live in their retirement years.

Helen's loneliness was compounded by her learning disability. She felt different from the other children; she felt dumb. She tried so hard, but she just couldn't get her brain to do what she wanted. Her grandparents lacked the patience to work with her. She rarely saw her father throughout her life. When he remarried, had children, and moved back to her hometown, she was not included in his new family.

Painful relationships became a pattern in her life. One day she met a man through her work. She was flattered that he paid attention to her and wanted to spend time with her. She fell "hook, line, and sinker" in love with him. She gave herself totally to him. As he was a police officer, she didn't question his unavailability at times. When he stood her up, work was always the reason. As one year rolled into another, she wondered if he was ever going to make a commitment of marriage to her. Then the inevitable happened. She found out he was married, and with a family all along. When she confronted him, he became enraged and physically abused her. She was so starved for love and attention that she continued in this abusive relationship for many years.

I would suggest that he was a picture (in her childhood heart) of what she thought her father was like. The military father was represented in the police officer, also a father. She loved her father and longed for his love and affection, but she also hated him for cruelly abandoning her. Abandonment was the worst fear in her heart and mind, so she put up with the abuse from the

90

married man. She had the same love-hate relationship with him that she had with her father.

Although Helen was faithful to the religious tradition in which she was raised, she seldom found comfort in it. In time, however, she was invited to a Bible study in another church, and there she saw a woman who modeled something she knew she didn't have. This Bible teacher was also a Christian counselor. She began to impart hope. Helen looked forward to the time spent in counsel and prayer with this woman; it became like a lifeline. There she found a personal love relationship with the Son of God, Jesus Christ. This newfound friend, Bible teacher, counselor, and mentor became like a spiritual mother. Helen went from being like a tightly bound bud to a full-bloom flower. Her life gave forth a fragrance of caring for others, especially the hurting.

God redeemed the pain of Helen's life by equipping her to minister to others. In time, she opened her home for a Bible study. She became like a spiritual mother to a group of hurting women. She passed on what God had done for her. Today, she is one of the most caring and sensitive people I know. Is it any wonder that Helen's spirit would turn around and flee back into the womb, not wanting to be born? Just look at the pain and rejection that awaited her. The following prayer is similar to what she prayed with her prayer counselor:

Father God, I acknowledge that You are the Life-Giver, and my life was not a mistake or an accident. Forgive my rebelliousness in not wanting to be born. Forgive my response to rejection, for fleeing back into the womb and fleeing from life. Synchronize my spirit with Your Spirit so that I may move in Your timing and have my being in You. Set my mind free of the distortions and misconceptions that contribute to my learning difficulty. Set my spirit right; rewire my brain so that it functions the way You designed. May Your Spirit of truth come in to bring to death the lies I have believed from the womb and throughout my life. I

91

agree with Your Word that I am fearfully and wonderfully made. I choose to embrace life! In Jesus' name. Amen.

I (Shelvy) had a faulty message written on my heart about life because of the prenatal wound of rejection, the wound against my sexuality at birth, the learning disability, and the childhood sexual abuse, My responses to my woundedness contributed to this message. My heart acted like a magnet that drew to myself a husband who would reinforce all the lies I believed. Rejection followed me like a stray animal seeking shelter in my wounded heart, and it would take more transforming love to remove both the lies and my negative responses.

Chapter 5: It's Never Too Late to Have a Happy Childhood

Mr. Performer

Ever since I was a child, I (Jim) had a love of God and a deep searching to know Him more. As a devout Catholic boy, I endeavored to perform all I learned that was needful for my faith to work. It's interesting that as a teen I was a newspaper boy for years, delivering the Brooklyn Daily Eagle newspaper to about seventy families daily in their urban apartments in Brooklyn, NY. I was a faithful adherent to all the functions of my church: Mass, confession, sacraments, prayer and abstinence—but it just hadn't accomplished all I was working to attain. Like all those stairs I endlessly climbed as a newspaper delivery boy under my own power, all the striving served a good purpose but left me tired out. There had to be more, a joy that I had not experienced with all my performing.

Much later at the end of 1974, to the surprise of all, I severed all ties with my former life. I left my wife, family, home, job and many friends. In my shame I remember asking God that I not lose my "faith"—my connection to Him (as I then knew it). I had purposed to move out, to the shock and hurt of many, (please forgive me) and find a "better life." My children were mostly grown when I left. It took five years of the Lord working in my heart, to bring me to a place of willingness to go back. When I sought reconciliation, my former wife informed me that she had found another and was remarrying. I later found out the wedding took place six days after I spoke to her. I see now how important it was to respond to the Lord's leading at the time.

I still brought my need to perform correctly with me. You can decide to change the scenery of your life but you still bring your character and habits of life with you. As a result, you reap the same—or worse—fruit. God can bring us out of an Egypt of enslavement, but we still need to let him take the Egypt out of us. Through it all, the Lord would eventually work in me a willingness to enter His rest.

I knew my life's "performance" had been successful to all outward appearances. We had a lovely, five-bedroom ranch home in a Connecticut suburb, an acre of lawn on a beautiful pond with trees and gardens, along with the respect of the community and our church. We were active in local church functions. I had worked at my schooling, an engineering degree, followed by business courses. I was then president of a nationally known design-consulting firm.

But it wasn't enough.

We lived in lovely, comfortable circumstances, yet I was still filled with strife. You can obtain much by hard work and still have little. There had always been that fruitless motive underneath: Just a little more and we'll be happy. Tomorrow has to get better! Life was a performance seemingly demanded by many. Or so I believed. I couldn't be real since I was always performing or acting to succeed with everyone around me. So I couldn't be intimate or open with anyone either. As a part of the performance, the striving, I could let no one in. I heard a young, recently popular, award-winning actor say that he didn't want to give interviews because that would allow people to know him too well. "If they know me too well then, I won't be asked to play other character parts."

Similarly, if I don't let you know the real me, then I can perform to suit the occasion or my needs, never letting you close to that "hidden me." It's that desire to perform to try to control how others respond to me that is so destructive to relationships and intimacy with others. If we strive to please men, we're putting God last. We never will live out of our real center. We are left unloved for ourselves and unable to love unconditionally. Everything we do then has a hidden agenda. Simply put, the agenda is: Please love my performance so I can feel that I am loved as a result.

We tell others that if you steal you will be stolen from. I had stolen from my former wife and family. So a year or so after leaving, I found myself assuming all the family's credit card debts and having creditors on my back. I was living in a tiny cottage in the woods with two cats as companions and having a difficult time making a living. My former wife now had the responsibilities of the children (two away at college and two at home), the family house, and her own struggles. I was doing private design and engineering consulting with various clients and struggling to keep my head above water. Family support payments had fallen behind. In all this the Lord was working to bring me to the end of myself.

When I first left my family and home, I found, through a pastor friend, a rent-free house-sitting job in a mansion. I lived there sequestered away for seven or eight months. The owner had died suddenly at seventy years of age and was found by the housekeeper under the grand piano upon her arrival on Monday morning. He was the seventh child of the seventh generation of a wealthy top industrialist who had founded one of the largest long-standing corporations of today. His sister, the sixth child, needed someone to watch over the private estate home until other arrangements were made. I believe the Lord was gently rubbing my nose in it as I took in these surroundings and began to realize the loneliness of his life. He had been in Broadway production design as the stage manager of some well-known and successful musicals and had a couturier of friends numbering

95

Broadway's famous. With his family's ultra-wealth, he had a seven-bedroom, five-bath residence located on the harbor in one of the wealthiest towns in his county. It was complete with an Olympic-size swimming pool and a cultivated, prize garden complete with three-tiered fountain.

The house was loaded with antiques, including the previous century's finest furnishings that money could buy. Most had been inherited from the grandparents' estate or collected from all over the world in the owner's travels. He had forty-eight place settings of the finest china and expensive solid silverware. Despite all this, I believe he lived a lonely life and in the end, died alone. Like me, he was in the performing business—on Broadway rather than the corporate world.

It was in this setting that I learned the empty dryness of wealth that is amassed for self. The Lord seemed to say, "Jim, do you want to have your life end like his, all alone in the midst of great lifeless acquisitions, a performer in the midst of expensive scenery without an audience that cares about you?"

It was in a subsequent, simple, one-bedroom cottage that I found even greater truths. I was still seeking. I regularly attended a new and different denomination church, and I had begun watching televangelists. One in particular, who regularly focused on God's unconditional love, really reached me on the heart level. I realized how much I had assumed that God was a great taskmaster who would never be satisfied with my performance, no matter how great. "I knew you were a hard man and I was afraid...so I hid your talent" (Matthew 25:24). I had cast Father God in the image of my alcoholic, controlling father whom I could never please. I never received any approval from him. I had buried my true self in performance. I had been striving to gain acceptance all my life, when all the while it was there but I hadn't believed it.

I began seeking more biblical truth, studying God's Word daily. I consumed books and tapes on faith questions. I studied under some good biblical teachers for years. Prayerfully, I also began to make large sacrifices from my limited resources to contribute to God's work. At that time I believe the Lord lead me to start visiting and ministering in prisons. From this I subsequently realized that I was a prisoner the Lord wanted to set free. "Give and it will be given unto you..." (Luke 6:38). If I needed true freedom, then I needed to help others in Christ be free.

Holy Roller or Easy Roller

At one point I (Jim) had made a bid for a large job with a personal care products company in Boston. I knew I had the unique talent needed. The product was brand new in concept and design. The project was to develop a personal hair-care appliance that would require capable product-design engineering and industrial design. The end result would be an attractive consumer product. This was the unique combination of skills in which I had experience. But seven firms were competing for the program. I badly needed the revenue to confront my heavy debt burden and the creditors who were reaching the end of their patience. I labored at preparing the bid proposal, knowing I could receive a sizeable down payment right away if I landed the work. I was really sweating the outcome.

The product manager had told me that he would call Monday at 3:30 p.m. to let me know either way. As the time approached, I got on my knees and did something I now realize was necessary and powerful but that I had never quite done before: I gave God the choice! I told Him my dire need for money. The creditors were threatening. "If I don't get this work, I'm going down the drain pipe. But, Lord, if that's where You're going to be that's where I want to be. I want Your will done even though You know I believe I need this work."

The phone rang at that exact moment, and when I picked it up the product manager, without an introduction, said, "You got it." I had won the bid, but more importantly God had told me, "You got it." In other words, learn to always give your will to Him so He can bring His power to bear for your best. God looks to bestow His power where we are surrendered completely to Him.

We now have a stained-glass plaque that hangs in our kitchen window that says, "God gives the best to those who leave the choice to Him."

"For the eyes of the Lord run to and fro throughout the whole earth, to show Himself strong on behalf of those whose heart is loyal to Him" (2 Chronicles 16:9). That work went on for over a year and a half until the product was introduced nationally on the consumer market. I had learned to give my will over to God in a new and greater way, to cease my striving. I had decided to follow the Holy Spirit, rather than be a holy roller struggling under my own power to perform. I wanted to rest in His decisions for my life, rather than to struggle to obtain my own.

As a little boy, I felt more constrained by the fear of punishment than by any other force. Due to my father's alcoholism, punishment often came for reasons I couldn't begin to understand. Mostly there was verbal abuse but at times the abuse was physical. (Abuse, in our judgment, goes beyond a corrective swat or a spanking when needed.)

My mother had a deep fear of my father doing serious damage to me even before I was born. But she tempered her interference, thinking it could increase his rage toward me. I tried to always please him. I believed my father was a good man inside and that alcohol was the problem. I just couldn't figure out why I couldn't seem to satisfy him, even when he was sober.

So I'd try harder, only to seemingly fail again. As any child might do in that situation, I judged myself as bad or unlovable. There was just some bad part of me I couldn't identify or correct. How could even God love me or want me to love Him the way I am?

"I get it … God will love me if I just fix myself up." Having a vow that denied the possibility of unconditional love, I began a life-long habit of performance orientation—I felt I had to earn all love through my performance.

Every child, even as an infant, has suffered rejection on occasion out of no fault of its own. But when the child takes on guilt, or shame, at feeling unloved or not nurtured, trouble is exacerbated. *It's my fault things aren't going well* (guilt). Or *There are things about me that must be unlovable* (shame). So even as children, we decide to build walls around our inner selves to keep out rejection and pain. These walls are built over time to keep people away and to escape from the hurt. Ultimately they are built to prevent others from seeing those mysterious parts the child believes make him or her unlovable, or worthy of rejection.

I build these walls using many various forms of escape. Keep in mind that, while these activities may be harmless in themselves, the real problem is my inner heart's motivation: *If anything good (loving) is to happen to me, I have to make it happen myself!* That is, I must be in control. I control everything by what I do. I must even control those things outside of me that are not mine to control. (Good luck! How's it working for you? It didn't for me, but I still thought it was the only show in town.)

Even as very little ones, in our experience of rejection we start building walls around ourselves to keep out pain. The walls are formed by little inner vows like, *I'll never get caught doing that again,* or *I'll never let anyone see that part of me.* These walls are meant to protect us from more pain, but they also prevent us from receiving love. With each hurt, we only build them higher. (See Figure 1.)

Figure 1

So the inner pain or emptiness becomes walled in and never is processed or healed. As though suffering with a wound that's covered over and never attended to, we're hurt and closed off to receiving truth in our inner being. Every wound is healed from the inside out, not from the outside in; ask your doctor.

But I still need to feel loved. So I continue to go about performing and "doing" to earn rewards. I've become a "human doing" rather than a human being. (See Figure 2.)

The self I now present to others is not the real me, but a marionette to please or control how others respond to the perceived me. This is not self-control, which is a fruit of the Spirit. My very being or true identity is hidden. I practice controlling the image I want to present for your approval and love. I call this image my "I-doll." I spend all my time worshipping this image for what it can achieve for me. This is idolatry. The trouble with anything I worship other than God is that it makes me just like it: deaf and dumb.

Figure 2

If you in turn show love to my straw doll, I never receive it behind my walls. I think you only loved a performance and not me. So I grow lonelier and lonelier, striving to perform better and better. As I start out, I'm under many self-imposed rules, such as "be neat," or "be quiet," or "never get angry—then I'll be loved."

As I grow older, I become more adept at living under the ever-revised rules so you'll appreciate me. Just show me the rules that will induce you to respond to me correctly as I perform them. I don't want an open relationship. That's full of fear. I don't want to be corporate with you. I want to control you so you'll always like me. Just tell me what you want.

Inevitably when I seek a relationship with God, I am still asking Him to just give me the rules. *You wouldn't want to talk to the real me if you knew me. Tell me how to perform so I can get You to dance for me.*

An actor on stage and his audience are both relating to the role that he is playing, not to each other personally as individuals. So our audience and we, too, can only be relating to our variously conjured "I-dolls." We never really know one another. I believe this was what Jesus spoke of in Mathew 7:21-23, when they said "'Lord, Lord, have we not prophesied in your name?' And then I will declare to them, 'I never knew you, depart from Me you who practice lawlessness.'" They were performing to a set of rules while never relating to Him personally. Consequently He never knew them.

We can use good rules for our own ends and wind up with fruitless lives. If I love what others think of me, I will never really love them or receive their love in turn. I remember one time entering a pew to sit and asking the Father, "How am I doing?" He replied, "Don't ask Me how you are doing, rather, ask Me what I am doing." Jesus said, "I only do what I see the Father doing" (John 5:19). That's a relationship you can build on. When you are dedicated to following the Father's lead, you are building an eternal relationship—one of giving yourself away to God, knowing His unconditional love, loving Him and others first.

The old reasoning said, "If you notice and reward me, you must love me, right?" So I seek attention first, rather than love. This is the devil's workshop. He loves drawing attention for himself to bolster his pride. The result is that I (like him) don't let you see the inner me. More and more, I disconnect myself from the inner me. So if you want me to be smart, I'll learn to act smart. If you want me to be quiet, I'll put on my quiet costume and mask. If the boss wants me to be neat, I'll be a "neat freak" as long as you'll reward me, notice me, focus on me, and give me your attention. I might even think that you love me, but I'm actually about bolstering my own pride.

So I go about following whatever rules, laws, or regulations you seem to require. I've given control of my life to whoever will seem to care about me. Naturally, I gain many rewards, because as I do well I am rewarded. But my heart is full of quiet desperation and loneliness. No one knows the real me, only the "performer." As I sow I will reap in kind, but the one being rewarded is my puppet doll, my "I-doll" of self, not the real (empty) me.

People may desire the performance, but that's not the true me they are seeing, only the performer. We are like the young actor we mentioned previously, who didn't want people to know the real him through interviews since it would limit the number of roles he'd be offered. If you don't know me, then I'm free to play any role I want, even false ones to gain seeming acceptance. I'm striving to be in control of every moment. And the carefully hidden me never receives real love or acceptance. I may evolve a greater and greater need to control you, becoming more and more angry when your response is not the desired one. Fear becomes surrounded by hardened walls of anger to keep you under my control.

Intimacy (into-me-see) is lost along with the possibility of true deep relationships when we practice performance orientation. People say to you, as they have me (Jim), "I don't really know you." All they were seeing was my performance, not the real me. I appeared to have it all together. Some were shocked to find out truths about my childhood or inner fears. To others I appeared to be standoffish or snobbish, although I remained unaware of their assessments. I was deceived in thinking I was connecting (relating) with my performances, but my heart was hidden.

103

We've hurt ourselves, others, and God by our wrong choices. Ultimately, Jesus took all guilt and shame to the cross. He's the only one who is able to take upon Himself our guilt—or another's. Only He can handle our guilt, because He was guiltless. He can free us from guilt and the true shame of our wrongdoing or sins. Guilt or shame can only rightly be handled as we seek forgiveness from those we've harmed, first from God and then, in love, from others.

When my mom, and several nuns, taught me about heaven and hell, I had another reason to fear punishment: God! I'd have to be good in order to please Him, too. I didn't want to go to hell. I readily accepted the lie that God's love was conditional. I'd have to perform correctly to be loved by Him! Fear of punishment and fear of people's opinion of us are two of satan's major weapons. He uses these to block and eventually destroy our relationship with God.

I loved Jesus and told Him so when receiving my first Communion at seven years of age. I remember saying, "I want to be good all my life and be with You, Jesus, when I die." Not a bad desire for a faith life, but I didn't realize only He could accomplish that in me. However, I used that desire to motivate my performance orientation that started with *make sure you don't die with a big mortal sin on your soul if you want to get to heaven.* I didn't realize that only God's goodness could save me, not my own performance of good. My picture of Father God was of Him placidly looking down from heaven with a clipboard recording all my deeds, good or bad. These records would be used in a dramatic reckoning when I finally arrived there for judgment. Such fearful anticipation is also how I envisioned my relationship with my earthly father.

I believed that if I were able to go to confession just before dying, then my sins would be forgiven and I'd arrive with a good record. If not, then I was going to the fires for all eternity, or maybe for just a little while if they were tiny sins. Meanwhile, God would be the silent observer who might gaze down heaven's parapets at me once in a while. He might even sprinkle some "twinkle-dust"— to empower me to do well. But doing or being good was mainly my responsibility. I believed His love was to be earned by me. So I became a star on the empty treadmill of performance. How well I performed, I thought, would eventually earn me more and more acceptance, completeness, and love.

And so at forty-two, I found myself being successful, as many considered me to be. I was tired and empty. I had been striving but never fully obtaining the love I needed. How could I, when the hardened belief of the little boy inside was that he was unlovable? So I kept up the walls of pride, not believing unconditional Love was there working and seeking to knock my walls down. I walked away from it all—wife, family, job, friends, and community. Interestingly, the year before, a design concept of mine was published in a leading national financial magazine. The article did a good job of foreshadowing things to come for both me and for our culture. Various top design firms across the country had been asked to prophesy what the future held for American consumers in the way of design and invention. My idea was elaborated on, complete with various drawings as a "Fully Automated, Totally Enclosed Self-Cleaning Toilet" facility. It was the featured design for the survey article. It conceptualized through illustrations. It described a washroom that would be used in future public installations. You were assured as the reader that, by automatic means, the facility would totally scrub, sanitize, drain, and air-dry its every surface periodically on a self-programmed basis. I was quoted in the article talking of the public's often-unfortunate tendency to desire in a product less than the best at a cheaper price. I had said, "The public is more inclined toward throwing away last year's model for the newest fad or fashion rather than paying a premium for good quality and or durability."

What was interesting about the Lord's inspiration coming to me to visualize such a concept was that shortly after, we all found ourselves captivated by "self-help." We were all looking for ways to clean up our lives. Many of us without the Lord's help. Give me the latest word on how I can fix up my own act! Books, television, the media were awash with many approaches to filling this urge in us to clean up our own "toilet." "Tell me how to perform better. What I've tried hasn't worked well for me so far."

We draw to ourselves a life that reflects the inner beliefs written on our hearts. But until we allow God to change our hearts through complete death to our faith in our own ability to heal our hearts, we will find ourselves performing again and again for all the wrong reasons. Galatians 2:20 says, "I have been crucified with Christ, it is no longer I who live, but Christ lives in me; and the life I live in the flesh, I live by faith in the Son of God who loved me and gave Himself for me." Not only will the marionette, the lifeless "I-doll" I created have to go, but so will the old walled-in self with its foolish vows and expectations have to die. What I needed was a good funeral, followed by resurrection to a life of faith in Him. Thankfully, in Jesus Christ this has been accomplished for us all. Our job is to grab on to this faith in our day-to-day walk.

Overcoming "performance orientation" by ourselves is impossible. It is much like asking myself, how do I cast away my fears? I can perform as if they're not there, but I can't make them disappear. For many of us, this is the only strategy we know. Can you see that, while ignoring the fear at the root of all "performance orientation" could be thought to be a good thing, it doesn't solve the inherent problem? I'm acting out of fear, not faith. I'm living under the law of the "man rules" I think will gain your favor. I still have to put on an act. It doesn't break down the fear-filled walls of isolation (Figure 1) built over years of manipulating others with my "I-doll."

For years, as we counseled and asked the Lord how we should pray during a session for a performance-oriented person, the Holy Spirit would prompt us not to pray, or would rather lead us to be unspecific in our prayers. The Lord knew that the counselees would take the prayer as a "to-do" list and go about trying to perform what we'd pray for them. We would be giving them more new rules or laws to adopt.

The answer to "performance orientation" or "What-should-I-do?-ism," is found in the Bible: "Perfect love casts out all fear" (1 John 4:18). Jesus has to replace the fear in our hearts with His perfect love. Then we will have no need to perform for Love. He will be a part of us in this area of faith as well.

Every year we ask the Lord to give each of us (Shelvy and me) a particular scripture for that year. We meditate on that scripture for the Lord to do His work in us that year. Several years ago, He gave me the scripture, "If you love Me, you will keep My commandments" (John 14:15). My first response was my usual, "But why, Lord? I know that scripture well, as many do. If I love you, I'll try to keep your commandments?"

"Not exactly, Jim. Think about it some more."

As I did, I began to see that the Lord wanted my focus to be first on loving Him. Out of that would come my obedience to His commands. Not striving to perform the rules—that moves my focus off of Him onto His rules. That would make the commandments my god, not God, Himself. Jesus said that to love God with our whole heart, soul and mind and to love our neighbor as ourselves are the greatest commandments, from which the entirety of the law and the prophets (the Old Testament) follows. See Mathew 22:36-40 and Mark 12:28 and on. Loving Him and my neighbor is foremost. He came that we might fulfill all the commandments in Him.

"Without Me you can do nothing" (John 15:5).

Complete or Compete

During most of my high school years, I (Shelvy) had a reoccurring dream. I was attending a school that had three floors. I was on the first floor when I would leave one class and hurry to my locker to get my book for the next class. I couldn't get the combination right and the locker wouldn't open. I was standing there trying to decide what to do: Go to the office for the correct combination and be late for the next class, which was at the other end of the school and all the way to the third floor, or go to the next class and be on time but without the right book for the class and hope that the teacher didn't find out. I would wake up in a panic.

This dream was a reflection of the anxiety I experienced trying to do the right thing and stay out of trouble. Part of this anxiety was due to my trying to live up to the high standard set by my older sister. She was my role model; I admired her and wanted to be just like her. It wasn't her fault that I felt measured by her. It would be years later before I learned an important lesson: we compete when we don't feel complete! When the "L" is missing we feel incomplete, and to me that "L" represents Love. I didn't feel loved and I didn't love myself.

So I was set on a path to compete and perform well. Always trying to be perfect, I felt like a failure. Since I never could attain the high standard I set for myself, I was prone to depression. But that just added to the pressure to perform well and keep smiling even though I felt like I was dying inside. I certainly couldn't let anyone know I was depressed.

I was voted for many offices in the student government and various clubs but none of it ever satisfied me. I still can't believe my graduating class voted for me to give the commencement speech on their behalf. And then, they honored me by voting me the girl "Most Likely To Succeed." I graduated feeling that I had fooled everyone, because I knew I really was dumb and no one would like me if they really knew me. Such was the war that raged inside of me.

I carried over the same attitudes in my Christian walk. I served on multiple committees, sang in the choir, taught every age group in Sunday school from toddlers to adults, and volunteered for whatever needed doing. I love to study the scriptures, so I would read the Bible through each year in a different translation. I tried to perform for God just like I had done all my life.

It was during a period of time when I was doing a study on the Old Testament tabernacle of Moses that I made a life-changing discovery. There are about fifty chapters in scripture that give details as to how the tabernacle was to be built and used. This included all the furniture and the priests' garments. As I read the chapters, I would take notes and savor the beauty and wonder of it all. But while I was doing this study, something else was taking place in my life. It seemed like overnight, I woke up to a rash under my arms. It was red and I couldn't put any deodorant on because it made the burning worse.

In the course of my busy days, I would perspire. Not only was this unsightly, but I was ruining my clothes. Out of desperation, I went to the doctor. He told me I was allergic to some ingredient in my deodorant and to stop using it until the rash cleared up. So I went home armed with a medicated cream to solve the rash problem. But my problem was long from being solved. Once the rash cleared up, I tried one product after another but to no avail; I soon broke out from each one of them. It didn't matter if they were the drugstore variety or the expensive department store fare. What was I to do?

It was about this time that I discovered in my study of the Old Testament priests' garments, that "They shall have linen turbans on their heads and linen trousers on their bodies; they shall not clothe themselves with anything that causes sweat" (Ezekiel 44:18).

I could hardly believe my eyes! I didn't even know the word "sweat" was in the Bible, except where it says Jesus sweat drops of blood. And sweat was what was causing me so much trouble right now. I know there are no coincidences in my life, only God-ordained incidences. If the Lord didn't want the priest working up a sweat as they served Him in the Tabernacle and, thus, soiling their priestly garments, was He asking the same of me? So, there was only one thing for "Miss Perform Perfectly" to do: repent!

I don't know how long I spent on my knees repenting. My list kept growing longer and longer. I began to catch a glimmer of how much I had grieved the heart of the Lord with all my striving. He didn't want me rushing around, trying to accomplish a dozen things at one time. I didn't have to prove my worth to Him. If I were feeling driven, it wasn't the Lord doing the driving. I was clearly the one behind the wheel.

I have heard it said that the shepherd goes before the sheep and leads the way. But it is the butcher that is behind the sheep, driving them to slaughter. He wanted me to move in His time, be led by His Spirit, and with His grace upon me. A gracious woman—that is what He wanted me to be!

Of course, you guessed it: As soon as I learned this lesson, I was able to go back to using my same favorite deodorant and have never had a rash again. I have come to love Matthew 11:28-30: "Come to Me, all you who labor and are heavy laden, and I will give you rest. Take My yoke upon you, and learn from Me, for I am gentle and lowly in heart, and you will find rest for your souls. For My yoke is easy and My burden is light."

I found what God thinks about success in Joshua 1:8: "This Book of the Law shall not depart from your mouth, but you shall meditate in it day and night, that you may observe to do according to all that is written in it. For then you will make your way prosperous, and then you will have good success."

I want to be found pleasing unto the Lord and hear Him say, "Well done, good and faithful servant." Let's see what the Bible says about anxiety or being anxious:

"Search me, O God, and know my heart, try me, and know my anxieties; and see if there is any wicked way in me, and lead me in the way everlasting" (Psalm 139:23-24).

"Anxiety in the heart of man causes depression, but a good word makes it glad" (Proverbs 12:25).

In Luke 12:22-34, Jesus exhorts us: "Do not worry" (v. 22). "And which of you by worrying can add one cubit to his stature? If you then are not able to do the least, why are you anxious for the rest?" (v. 25-26). "But seek the kingdom of God, and all these things shall be added to you. Do not fear, little flock, for it is your Father's good pleasure to give you the kingdom" (v. 31-32).

Jesus tells us not to worry and not to fear. Later in Philippians 4:6-7 we read: "Be anxious for nothing, but in everything by prayer and supplication, with thanksgiving, let your requests be made known to God; and the peace of God, which surpasses all understanding, will guard your hearts and minds through Christ Jesus."

[I realize that some who are reading this may suffer from a diagnosed anxiety disorder, and perhaps you are dependent upon medication to keep the anxiety from overwhelming you. This is not a lack of faith on your part, but obedience in caring for yourself. Too many Christians have felt stigmatized for taking medication. Please know that "There is therefore now no condemnation to those who are in Christ Jesus, who do not walk according to the flesh, but according to the Spirit" (Romans 8:1). Many suffer from chemical imbalance, and it manifests itself in various disorders. Until Jesus heals you and it's verified by your physician, stay on the medication and continue to let the Wonderful Counselor work with you to make you whole. We have seen many who have religious pride that refuse to be treated with medication. Be careful that you don't dictate to God how He should heal; that would be putting yourself in God's place.]

The question before us is, are we striving to compete, doing things on our own, or are we willing to choose to believe that we are complete in Him and submitting ourselves to His process?

"As you therefore have received Christ Jesus the Lord, so walk in Him, rooted and built up in Him and established in the faith, as you have been taught, abounding in it with thanksgiving. Beware lest anyone cheat you through philosophy and empty deceit, according to the tradition of men, according to the basic principles of the world, and not according to Christ. For in Him dwells all the fullness of the Godhead bodily; and you are complete in Him, who is the head of all principality and power" (Colossians 2:6-10).

"All Scripture is given by inspiration of God, and is profitable for doctrine, for reproof, for correction, for instruction in righteousness, that the man of God may be complete, thoroughly equipped for every good work" (2 Timothy 3:16-17).

Overcoming

"These things I have spoken to you, that in Me you may have peace. In the world you will have tribulation; but be of good cheer, I have overcome the world." (John 16:33).

The word "tribulation" means to press, afflict, that which occasions distress, trouble or vexation; severe affliction.[15] This word is used to describe crushing grapes or olives in a press.

Most hurtful life experiences could be classified under one of those definitions for the word "tribulation." And Jesus said He has overcome all of it. What does that mean to us today?

"For whatever is born of God overcomes the world. And this is the victory that has overcome the world our faith. Who is he who overcomes the world, but he who believes that Jesus is the Son of God?" (1 John 5:4-5). Today, believe that Jesus is the Son of God, put your faith in Him!

"Yet in all these things we are more than conquerors through Him who loved us" (Romans 8:37).

---

15. Webster's Collegiate Dictionary, s.v. "tribulation."

112

The Greek word for the phrase "more than conquerors" is hupernikao.[16] We are conquerors, champions, and victorious people. God says we are even more than that: We are more than conquerors; over and beyond! I would suggest that we are super-overcomers in Christ Jesus. We have overcome what the world has dished out to us, (whatever hurts have come our way) because Jesus Christ, the Son of God, loves us! His love covers a multitude of sins and His love never fails.

So, "Beloved One," walk just as He walked, for you are more than an overcomer. "Do not be overcome by evil, but overcome evil with good" (Romans 12:21).

You may want to pray this prayer for the overcoming of performance orientation:

Lord, You have opened my eyes to see my striving... my performing to be accepted. Forgive me for the wrong motives for what I do. Forgive me for believing the lies that I must perform correctly to be good enough to be loved and accepted. Forgive me for living for the approval of others rather than believing in Your unconditional love and acceptance of me.

Bring to death in me the habits, structures of thinking, and ways of performing with wrong motives. I choose to believe "When a man's ways are pleasing to the Lord, He makes even his enemies to be at peace with him" (Proverbs 16:7).

I choose this day to rest in You, my Lord God Almighty, and believe in Your love for me. Thank you for setting me free of performance orientation! In Jesus' name, Amen.

I (Jim) have a large blue button that says, "It's Never Too Late To Have A Happy Childhood." Thanks to the Lord Jesus Christ, that statement is true. We are all a work in progress, and He

---

16. *Strong's Exhaustive Concordance*, s.v., G5245, "hupernikao."

promises in Philippians 1:6: "Being confident of this very thing, that He who has begun a good work in you will complete it until the day of Jesus Christ."

Chapter 6: Transformed by Love: Finding Our True Identity

Am I a Real Girl?

Linda was my (Jim's) fourth child and second daughter. She was born with cerebral palsy. She was classified as mentally retarded, although her greater problems were with cerebral palsy—motor skills limitations, her eyesight and extreme gastro-intestinal dysfunction were the bulk of the situation. (The G-I system had never correctly developed.) She was treated for this condition but suffered varying degrees of pain all of her twenty years. When I left my home, she was twelve and attending specials needs schools and group homes. When I had visitation rights, we'd do many of the single-father things together. I remember fondly the times we were together, though our conversations were usually limited as to subjects. She loved watching movies and would get me to do a imitations of her favorite movie characters over and over again, and we would laugh together.

One time I particularly remember her asking me a question in the midst of a crowded fast food place as we were eating our burgers. "How come you left us?" (in quite a loud voice.) It was like one of those old ads where everyone around us froze, as in a time warp, awaiting my response. I said, "I didn't leave you, I left your mom. I don't love her anymore, but I still love you." She didn't ask again. I now would say that I had decided not to love her mom anymore but wanted to still love my children as best I could. But "best I could" would have been to decide to continue to love my wife and them. There are no other solutions.

Studies have shown that parents are usually through the grieving process of a divorce in three to five years, but the children never adjust to the heartbreak of divorce throughout their entire lifetime. These studies also show that it's always better for the children if their parents remain together. God designed couples— one mother and one father—to love one another and, as the fruit of that love, to conceive, birth, and train up the children in unconditional love.

The Unexpected Legacy of Divorce offers the results of a twenty-five-year study on the subject of children of divorce. For the first time, using a comparison group of adults who grew up in the same communities, Judith Wallerstein and her research team, showed how adult children of divorce essentially view life differently from their peers raised in stable homes in which parents also confronted marital difficulties but decided to stay together. She shed light on the question so many parents confront: whether to stay unhappily married or to divorce. She says in her report, "Divorce is a cumulative experience. Its impact increases over time and rises to a crescendo in adulthood. In adulthood it affects personality, the ability to trust, expectations about relationships, and ability to cope with change."[17]

What's done to children, they will do to society. -Karl A. Menninger

---

When I (Jim) came into greater relationship with Jesus and His power in my life, I began a weekly chapel time, praying with Linda for her healing. One church's loving minister would pray

---

17. Judith Wallerstein, Julia M. Lewis, and Sandra Blakelee, *The Unexpected Legacy of Divorce,* (2000:New York, Hyperion), 298.

with me faithfully each week for a season. I did this with Linda for over a year. When I started, I was hopeful for her physical healing but I later understood that instead, God heard our prayers for total healing.

When I'd talk to Linda, she would sometimes ask me, "Am I a real girl?" I'd always answer, "Yes." Her condition, which we believe came from anoxia in a poorly performed "forceps" delivery, left her with distorted features, nervous motor skills, and thick glasses for nearsightedness. That caused others to stare and comment, which resulted in her questions. I believe her intelligence was there, although penned in by her physical problems.

A few teachers couldn't fit her into their mold and so rejected her. A few spent time loving her to life and accepting her unconditionally. I remember one such teacher, Mary, coming by the house with her boyfriend on a big black motorcycle to take Linda for a spin. The joyous look on Linda's face as she held onto those handlebars with her long blond hair streaming behind was unforgettable.

Each year I would buy a live tree at Christmas, then plant it afterward to represent each child. Linda's was the last planted. As they grew, they developed as much as the children did. Jimmy's tree was the first and grew tall, but Rick's grew taller, and so did he. Then there was Laureen's tree, and next there was Linda's, the smallest, but also kind of scrawny. Not as healthy, just like Linda. But you know, the birds always seemed to love Linda's tree. They would land on her raggedy branches.

Linda was love; plain old unconditional love. I don't know where she got it. Maybe it was learning to live with all the questions, with all the changes in her painful existence. She was loved, but somehow she learned to out-love us all. You should have heard her friends from her live-in group home talk of her love at her funeral in 1985.

She had given her life to the Lord a few years previously. We were at a Sunday morning service when an evangelist asked for all those who wanted Jesus in their hearts to stand. So I leaned close to Linda and asked her if she wanted Jesus in her heart and she said, "Yes," and I told her to stand. The evangelist asked, so I asked Linda, "Do you want to go forward to receive Jesus?" She went forward to repeat the prayer, asking Jesus to come and take over her life and her heart. I believe my prayers for her healing, along with others' prayers, had been answered. I knew now that Linda would be healed. The transformation had begun. I remember at the time that I felt she probably saw Jesus as an alien-like character. But I knew that her heart was right and that the Lord could work with that. Jesus meets us where we are. We have only to choose life with Him.

When I last saw Linda, she was with me for the weekend. We would drive around, and she would be the pilot and I would be the co-pilot steering the car. She'd say "right" and I would go right, "slow down" and I would slow down. I remember one time, just before the sun was setting and we had driven about forty miles from home, before I called it quits to go back home. The last Saturday, we both went to see a movie. I didn't suspect God's purposes in having us see this film at that time. The movie was about a toy puppet that desired to become a real child, not just a wooden puppet on strings.

When we got home from the movie, we ate dinner together and went to bed. Linda awoke in the middle of the night experiencing stomach pains, and I went in and sat beside her bed for a time. Later she called out to me again and asked that I sit and stay with her. It was a difficult night for Linda. I took her to her mother earlier than usual the following day. I had been sensitive to her diet and medication needs at the time, but thought perhaps something she had eaten might have disagreed with her.

The doctor saw her on Monday. They operated on her on Tuesday and found her intestines to be gangrenous.

She died on Wednesday and was with the Lord. She was a "real girl" at last. I believe there was a reason the Lord had arranged for us to see the movie that weekend. Through that timeless story, He confirmed both our hopes, that Linda would become the real person she always desired to be. Transformation complete!

Search for True Identity

So many times we have had a person sit across from us and say: "I don't know who I am. I've always done what I thought would gain me acceptance or approval, living to please others." It's exciting for us to watch their journey as God meets them with His love, a love that has the power to transform. Here is one such story:

Brett (we'll call him) arrived at our home in Connecticut after taking the train out of Manhattan. He was a personable young man in his 20s with bleached blond hair and very thin for his six-foot frame. He had recently made a serious commitment of his life to the Lord, and he knew he needed to make some changes. Brett was living in New York City, hoping for a career in acting. He had a degree in theater and had left the South after graduating from college, never wanting to return to the farm where he grew up. But after several years of mostly working as a waiter, he was discouraged. The theater scene wasn't exactly what he thought it would be. He met a lot of people who seemed willing to help him along his way but it was going to cost him. And it wasn't money they were after.

Brett had a wonderful sense of humor and we enjoyed his tales of growing up on the farm. He didn't like the farm life and never felt like he belonged. It was only when he was in high school that he felt he had found his place in acting. He told us "I never knew who I was, and through acting I could find identity, even if it was temporary." His parents had been past forty when they adopted him as a newborn.

119

As a teen, Brett struggled with sexual-identity confusion. He liked girls but mainly as friends. He was drawn to guys who were masculine, tall, and with dark hair. He never "acted out" until he reached New York. It usually started in a bar with a few too many drinks, and, before he knew it, he was in the "lifestyle," as he called it.

We laid out for Brett the work that we felt would have to be done for him to get free and find out his true identity. We agreed it would be very difficult for him to get healed and still live in Manhattan and associate with his old friends. Brett moved out of New York and took a job as a waiter while we worked with him. We grew to love him as a son. On his visits to our home, I would prepare some of the Southern foods (fried chicken, hush puppies, and sweet tea) that he missed from home. But his favorite dish was banana pudding. He had not had any since leaving the South.

In the course of prayer-counseling, Brett decided he wanted to find his birth mother and father. He was successful through the adoption agency in finding his birth mother. Of course he was nervous as he prepared to fly to the South to meet her for the first time. She was so different from anything he had imagined, it was hard for him to connect with her. She seemed too young. She had a houseful of children, and one of them said to him, "You're the lucky one—you got away!" He questioned in his mind if she could really be his birth mother. She was fifteen years old when she had become pregnant by her seventeen-year-old boyfriend. Her parents had immediately rushed her off to a home for unwed mothers several miles away. She never got a chance to tell her boyfriend that she was pregnant or even say good-bye. There was never a consideration that she could keep the baby because her parents said it was better to give it up for adoption as she was too young to raise a child.

Brett told us, "The one thing that made me know she was my mother was when she said that while she was pregnant she craved banana pudding."

He then asked about his father. She told him that when she returned from the home for unwed mothers, his family had moved away and she never heard from him again. She got out her high school yearbook and showed Brett a picture of his birth father. He was an athlete—muscular, masculine, with dark hair. The exact profile of the kind of guy Brett was always attracted to! Was Brett seeking his long-lost birth father, seeking that identification with him that he had never received? He couldn't identify with his adoptive father, who was a quiet, country farmer. He never received words of affirmation or physical affection from his adoptive father. That father had just left the raising of the boy to his mother. He saw even more clearly how he had been seeking his maleness in other males. He wanted from them what he sensed he lacked.

As we continued to work with Brett, we witnessed a wonderful transformation. Even his physical appearance and mannerisms changed and he became more masculine. He decided to move back home and accept his adoptive parents for who they were and be thankful for the life they had provided for him. In time, he started his own business and found that he really liked it and was very good at it. He flew back to see us and brought a wonderful young woman with him. He wanted us to counsel her and see how we felt about their combined backgrounds and the potential problems they might encounter. He had made a good choice; she knew the Lord and she loved Brett. We gave our blessings!

It has been a number of years since we have seen Brett, but our last communications revealed that God has blessed them with two healthy children, they were active in their church, and their business was going well. To God be the glory!

The Mirror of Truth

This story below is an allegory that demonstrates both the problem and the solution of the lack of healthy fathering:

"Once upon a time, a tiny, newborn lion cub was lying with his mother in the jungle, resting in the warmth of the sun and his mother's fur. Suddenly, without warning, a loud noise rang out among the trees and his mother jumped to her feet. Startled, the cub tumbled into a nearby brush, then watched as his mother fell to the ground and several other creatures, moving on only two legs, rushed in and seized her. Too frightened to move, he sat there, stunned, as the two-legged ones lifted his mother and disappeared into the forest.

"A strange and fearful silence fell over the area, and for a whole day the little cub would not move out from the brush where he hid. Finally, his stomach began to ache with hunger, and, seeing no movement in the area, he ventured out and walked unsteadily ahead, hoping to find something to eat.

"After some time, he came to a clearing and peered out from behind a leafy bush. Before him, in the middle of a lush, green meadow, were many other creatures—on four legs, with white, curly-bush skins, their heads bent low as they seized the grass with their teeth and chewed it. These creatures are eating, and they seem very peaceful, the cub thought to himself. Maybe they'll let me join them.

As he stepped out into the meadow, one of the larger creatures came over to greet him. At once, the cub poured out the sad story of his mother, and how hungry he was. 'You're welcome to stay and live with us,' the creature said. 'We're sheep, and we can teach you how to eat the grass.'

"The tired and lonely little cub was so encouraged by such warm hospitality that he thanked the sheep, and set about putting his teeth to the grass. Soon he noticed that the sheep had teeth that were different from his own; he had to work very hard to grasp the grass and chew it. Nevertheless, he was a hardy little fellow, and would not give up. Before long he had learned how to squeeze his jaws—painful though it was—so that he could pinch the grass and get it into his mouth.

"In fact, he became so fond of the sheep and so used to their company that he also learned how to open his mouth and make a 'baaa-a-a' sound; he even managed to prance somewhat with his wide, soft feet as they did with their small, hard hooves.

"Several years passed, and though he could never manage to eat, speak, or walk quite as the sheep did, the lion cub still enjoyed being a member of their family. In time, he even forgot his mother and the terror of his first days alive.

"One bright and sunny day, while the lion was grazing peacefully with his sheep family in the meadow, a loud and terrifying shriek suddenly burst forth from the mother sheep. Startled, he and the others stopped their grazing and looked up in alarm. 'Quick! Everyone into the forest at once!' the mother sheep shouted. And without thinking, all the others turned and followed her as she darted into the thicket.

"The young lion naturally turned to follow the sheep—but as he did, a strange impulse stopped him. 'What,' he wondered, 'was everyone so frightened of?' As he stood alone in the meadow, the mother sheep screamed at him one last time: 'Come with us immediately!' Again the lion turned—but again, he stopped. 'It's too late!' the mother sheep shouted. 'We must leave you behind!' And she disappeared into the woods.

"Alone and uncertain in the stillness of the warm afternoon, the lion puzzled over this strange turn of events. Shrugging his shoulders, he turned away from the forest where the sheep had run, and was about to bend down for another tear at the grass when suddenly his head jerked upright. A cold shiver of terror raced through his body as there, heading straight toward him—unhurried but deliberate—came a huge and mighty creature unlike any he had ever seen. Its feet were like huge, padded tree stumps; its teeth were long and sharp. 'How in the world,' the lion wondered, 'did this creature eat? Surely such teeth could not chew grass!' Behind the creature stretched a long, thick tail with a large tuft of hair at the end. What seized the young lion's attention, however, was the huge bush of hair surrounding the creature's head, waving majestically in the afternoon breeze.

"With its dark eyes riveted to his own, the creature lumbered toward the trembling young lion. The mother sheep, he realized in a moment of horror, was right. It was too late. Yet he was struck by a strange inner sense that held him there, even in his terror: he did not really want to run away from the creature. Indeed, he couldn't take his eyes off it.

"Then, at last, the creature stood before him. The young lion's legs were shaking as his wide eyes beheld this awesome figure. 'Follow me,' the creature said, his deep voice rumbling like a stormy sky.

As the creature turned and walked away, the young lion hesitated. Where in the world would it take him? An impulse arose to look over his shoulder to where the sheep had disappeared in the woods, but he checked it. He then stepped forward, following. For some time, the creature walked silently ahead. At first, the young lion tried to walk in its footsteps, but his sheep-prance kept him from doing so. Before long, though, he found himself leaping, stretching with surprising ease so that at times he even 'caught' the creature's wide-spaced footprints. Still, he could only wonder at how much smaller his own feet were. Leaping this way, the young lion was drawn up short—and stumbled clumsily—when the creature stopped and looked over its shoulder at him. 'Come here, beside me,' it said.

"Struggling quickly to right himself, the young lion stepped beside the creature, who now stood before a small pond deep in the forest. "Look down," the creature intoned, its rumbling voice echoing amid the trees. The young lion looked down. There, on the surface of the water, he saw a small creature beside a large one. Tentatively, he shook his head—and the head of the smaller creature shook too, stirring thin tufts of hair behind its ears. Puzzled, he drew back. And then it struck him. Hesitantly but deliberately, he leaned close to the water and looked again. Then slowly, he turned and looked at the creature towering silently above him. After a moment, he turned again to the water and stared intently.

"The forest hushed. At last, trembling, the young lion beheld the creature beside him. Lifting his head, he leaned back and thrust his sharp teeth at the treetops: 'R-R-R-O-O-O-A-A-A-R-R-R'"[18]

This allegory demonstrates what happens when there is not a father to model masculinity and affirm the son for who he is. The son is drawn to the woman, symbolized as a sheep. He models after her ways; walks as she walks, talks as she talks, and even, eats as she eats and what she eats. It is only as Jesus, the Lion of Judah, calls the son to follow Him that he learns to walk in His steps. The water represents the water of the Word where he may see that he is created in His image.

The same principles apply to daughters. They need both mother and father modeling healthy sexuality. If the mother models a life that says, "I'm a victim, I'm a doormat, it is not safe or fun being a female," the girl may quench her femaleness and determine that she doesn't want a life like her mother had. If the girl is molested or abused in some way, she feels it's not safe being a female. She feels unprotected and vulnerable. The message to her heart is "You can't count on the man, he won't be there for you. My father didn't protect me and no other man will either."

All these childhood wounds distort a child's concept of who God is and what He is like. Subconsciously, we project onto

---

18. Original author unknown.

Father God whatever our experience was with our earthly father. Until our minds are renewed with truth, we cannot know Him as He really is and we cannot become all we were meant to be.

Jesus is the supreme artist, more of an artist than all others, disdaining marble and clay and color, working in the living flesh. ~Vincent Van Gogh[19]

Father Hunger

"Although a mother's love and affirmation of a son or daughter is important in a thousand ways, she cannot finally tell her son that he is a man, nor her daughter that she is indeed a woman. There are a number of reasons why this is so, and why it is the father (or father substitute) who affirms sons and daughters in their sexual identity and therefore as persons. The most important one is that at puberty and adolescence, we are listening for the masculine voice. It is the strong, masculine love and affirmation coming through that voice that convinces us that we are truly and finally separate from our mothers."[20]

Because of the breakdown of fathering, sons and daughters don't know who they are and seek their identity in wrongful ways. Many precious sons of this nation have never been called forth to life by their fathers and therefore, are still attached to their mothers. They grew up only having their mother to affirm and bless them. Thus, they became "female-dependent" and, wherever that dependence is, there will be ambivalence toward the woman. He will love her, but also hate her. He loves her because she is there for him, but

19. Kathleen Powers Erickson, "From Preaching to Painting: Van Gogh's Religious Zeal, "*The Christian Century*. March 21-28, 1990, 300-302.
20. Leanne Payne, *Crisis In Masculinity*, (1985: Crossway Books), 15.

he will hate her because he needs her and fears he cannot make it without her and that she will control him. Thus, the ambivalence continues.

Prior to the Industrial Revolution, children worked alongside their fathers on farms and ranches across this nation and throughout most of the world. Fathers had opportunity on a daily basis to affirm their children and to bless them with a healthy, wholesome touch. Children drew strength from the presence of their father. They had a sense of security and well-being, because the family was together. They could settle down and identify with their father and grow and mature into the men and women God intended. But all of that changed when the father left to work in the factory or went off to war.

The number of children being raised in a single-parent home is increasing at an alarming rate. In the majority of these homes the single parent is the mother. Unfortunately, many fathers see their children only a limited amount of time after divorce, if at all. Addictions, alcoholism, and drug abuse among fathers have robbed many children of healthy fathering.

In *Sacred Romance* by Brent Curtis and John Eldredge, John writes of how he had a grandfather who stepped into his life when past hurts and wounds were about to take over, and during the years his father was battling alcoholism. He says his grandfather, "Pop," filled an empty place in his life. Pop became his hero, a cowboy and a gentleman in a cowboy hat and boots. Spending summers on his ranch was a schoolboy's dream—riding horses, chasing frogs, and all the things that a boy loves. He remembers riding with his grandfather in his old pickup, with his cowboy hat and leather work gloves, waving at nearly everyone on the road. At that time, folks waved back with respect. His grandfather filled the father-void.[21]

21. Brett Curtis and John Eldridge, *Sacred Romance,* (1997: Thomas Nelson Publishers), 36-37.

The apostle Paul reveals his paternal heart as he writes in 1 Corinthians 4:14-15, "I do not write these things to shame you, but as my beloved children I warn you. For though you might have ten thousand instructors in Christ, yet you do not have many fathers; for in Christ Jesus I have begotten you through the gospel." That warning is still going out to the Church today—"you do not have many fathers." We must do a better job of ministering to the fatherless!

⌒⌒

I am reminded of one spiritual father, Fred, who recently retired after influencing the lives of thousands of young people as the director of a Christian camp. One warm day in August, an organized activity for single parents brought some twenty-five single parents with more than fifty children to enjoy the recreation and spiritual nourishment so generously provided at the camp by Fred's capable staff. Shortly after they arrived, a single mom of four mentioned that her nine-year-old son wanted to "climb the mountain" like his big brother had done the year before, but he was afraid he wouldn't make it to the top. This kind of passing remark wasn't lost on a man like Fred.

The day before the traditional "climb of the mountain," all the youth were excited about the impending adventure. During one of the mealtimes, Fred took the opportunity to come up to the table and placed his hands on the nine-year-old boy's shoulders. "You're going to climb the mountain with us this year, aren't you?" he said. It was more than the words he spoke. Something in Fred's tone imparted strength to the boy. That encouraging tone along with his fatherly touch said, "I believe in you and I know you can do it." That small, informal gesture gave the boy the confidence to face down his fears and try. He was among the first group of kids who reached the mountaintop. He grew in leaps and bounds that day. A father-figure believed in him and thought he could make it to the top of the mountain. And he did!

Road Map to Transformation

Transformation isn't something that happens in just one moment. Rather, it's a journey, made of many moments. As we begin any path, we need a road map to help us reach our destination, and in this case the destination is our life destiny. God created us to not be "Lone Rangers" but enter into holy reliance on Him to reach that destiny. In other words, there's nothing wrong with asking for directions!

Proverbs 3:5-6 urges us to: "Trust in the Lord with all your heart, and lean not on your own understanding; in all your ways acknowledge Him, and He shall direct your paths."

What great news! He will direct our paths. Furthermore, He will be our personal guide; He will never leave us. Jesus also promises to complete the work that He's begun in us. God is the Faithful One and He will do it!

Let's look now at some of the road signs that have been posted to help guide us on this journey. We found it interesting, after writing the fourteen signposts listed below, that their number paralleled the fourteen Stations of the Cross. On closer look, we found even more detailed resemblance between the two. If you are unfamiliar with the Stations, they originated with a desire to reflect on Jesus' journey to the cross in a visual prayer pilgrimage, and they are used often by certain denominations, especially during Lent and times of repentance.

As a Catholic boy, Jim found that meditation on the Stations was a helpful way to learn of Jesus' suffering and grow closer to Him. Now, many years later, we have a beautiful wood carving of Station 11, showing Jesus from the perspective of the repentant thief hanging next to him. The plaque under it reads, "Jesus is nailed to the cross and yet reaches out to us in love."

While not all the Stations are found in Scripture, it is certainly Scriptural to take time to ponder the passion of Christ, asking God to use our imaginations to reveal Himself to us more deeply.

As you read through the Signposts, you may want to also look at the Stations of the Cross and compare each step along the way. However you wish to make your pilgrimage, remember that Jesus is the forerunner; He set the pattern for this transformational journey. While our sins are covered by the shed blood of Jesus, our sinful natures or habits need to be put to death on the cross. We are directed to the cross in more ways than one.

Signposts on the Road to Transformation

Signpost 1: Remember the Past

> Sometimes the memories are painful, but you have already lived through it and God will give you the strength you need to face it. You are not a child now, but an adult who is empowered with God's Spirit.

Station 1: Jesus Condemned to Death

> Facing the reality and the verdict of our past head-on can be painful; however, we can do so knowing that Jesus took it on in full. He was condemned so that we would not have any condemnation in Him. His death sentence not only frees us from the chains of our past, but also makes possible our life and future.

Signpost 2: Recognize What Went Wrong

> You can now bring a holy objectivity that you didn't have as a child. Because something bad happened to you, it doesn't mean you were bad. You need to see the difference between deliberate disobedience and innocence that has been violated.

Station 2: Jesus Carries the Cross

> Recognition is half of the battle, the first major step forward. It is the beginning of repentance, the beginning of the transformation

journey that will put the old patterns to death. As Jesus picked up that cross, He had already prayed in the Garden, already made up His mind to do the Father's will and received the verdict without flinching. Recognition implies our choice to submit our will to the to the truth of God.

Signpost 3: Responsibility for Your participation (Actions and Attitudes)

Own your own behavior and stop blaming others for what you did and thought. You aren't responsible for other's actions, but you are responsible for your responses! Identify the roots that produced the bad fruit. You are not being disloyal to your family of origin by remembering what happened and agreeing with God by calling some of their behaviors sinful. Parents are responsible to protect and provide for their children.

Station 3: Jesus Falls the First Time

We noticed that as Jesus fell three times, God addressed three ways in which we fall: Lust of the flesh, lust of the eyes, and the pride of life. He also addressed our triune nature: spirit, soul, and body. He took on our sins (sinful actions), our transgressions (rebellion), and our iniquities (sinful nature and ingrained patterns of dishonoring God). "Surely He has borne our griefs and carried our sorrows; yet we esteemed Him stricken, smitten by God, and afflicted. But He was wounded for our transgressions, He was bruised for our iniquities; The chastisement for our peace was upon Him, and by His stripes we are healed" (Isaiah 53:4-5).

With this first fall, the emphasis is on our sinful actions and responses. Instead of blaming others, acknowledging where we've fallen short helps position us to not only sin less but also see others with His perspective.

Signpost 4: Respond Differently Than You Did in the Past

While we cannot rewrite our history, we can choose to respond in light of the truth we now possess as adults about what happened.

131

Station 4: Jesus Meets His Mother

As Jesus met His mother, it was clear that their roles were in for a major change. We too will see family roles shifting as we put aside old ways of interacting. How we respond, especially to those with whom we grew up such as our mothers and fathers and those in authority, will greatly change as we allow God to work in us. Regardless of whether we meet them again personally, we "face" them again in a new light as we walk out our transformation.

Signpost 5: Repent for Your Sin

If God calls it sin, you should too! Don't justify your sin with self-righteousness or by taking vengeance into your own hands.

Station 5: Simon Helps Jesus Carry the Cross

Repentance is turning from our own ways to God's ways. Admitting we can't do it ourselves and learning to receive help is a pivotal part of repentance. Jesus demonstrated humility and holy dependence throughout His ministry, then again as He received the ministry of Simon's help.

Signpost 6: Receive Forgiveness and Absolution

Choose to forgive yourself. Don't try to be more holy than God. If He forgives you, receive it! Release your own self-hatred, and remember it is the shed blood of Jesus Christ that absolves you of your sin.

Station 6: Veronica Wipes the Face of Jesus

Receiving forgiveness and absolution is a washing, cleansing process, modeled so tenderly through Jesus' weakness and willingness to have His face wiped. Just hours before this cross walk, Jesus also allowed Mary of Bethany to wash His feet with her tears. Even though Jesus was without sin, He went before us in His demonstration of the need for cleansing, in both baptism at the start and in His last moments as women ministered to him.

Signpost 7: Release Forgiveness to Those Who Have Sinned against You

"Forgive even as I have forgiven you" (Colossians 3:13) and, if you want to be forgiven, you must choose, as an act of your will, to forgive.

Station 7: Jesus Fall the Second Time

We know we need to forgive, but we often don't want to. When we've been hurt we don't think of ourselves as being rebellious, but where we've been knocked down in life and then held grudges, we've taken on God's job. That load is too heavy for us to bear. Acknowledging those hurts and forgiving others ushers us from a position of rebellion to one in which we might receive His justice, righteousness, and peace.

Signpost 8: Reconcile with God and Others

Stop blaming God. He is not responsible for the exercise of each person's free will. And stop holding Him responsible for the reaping of bad fruit in your life. You sowed the seeds. Let Him lay the axe to those roots. Others have no more power in your life than you give them. See others as people valuable enough for Christ to die for. God said, "Be at peace with all men in so far as it concerns you" (Romans 12:18).

Station 8: Jesus Meets the Women of Jerusalem

The women of Jerusalem were among the few who did not reject Jesus during this horrendously disfiguring time. That kind of support, prayer, and unconditional love helps nurture us on the journey and emphasizes the importance of reconciliation on all levels. Fellowship needs to be restored both vertically (between us and God) and horizontally (between us and others) for complete healing to be manifested in our lives. The very structure of the cross gives us a picture of that convergence of heaven and earth.

Signpost 9: Restore Trust

It is the responsibility of the one who violated trust to begin a new track record of trust. But it's your responsibility to open your heart and determine to allow Jesus to restore your ability to trust. You with God, you with others, others with you.

Station 9: Jesus Falls the Third Time

Where we've fallen prey to wrong beliefs or been subject to lies and twists of the truth, God is true and reliable. Where we (or others) have been unfaithful and trust has been broken, He is faithful and trustworthy. It may take time for trust to be restored, but if we lean on Him, we will not stumble over someone else's shortcomings; if we lean on Him, we can also learn to walk in integrity and be true to our word.

Signpost 10: Refuse to rehearse the hurts of the past

If you have taken it to the cross in prayer, let it stay there. You do not need to be seen—or see yourself—as a victim. You are victorious in Christ. Don't keep making satan the center of your attention; rather, lift up the name of the Victor!

Station 10: Jesus' Clothes Are Taken Away

We need to participate in our own healing by actively taking off the old "garments." Where Jesus was completely stripped and appeared to be a helpless victim, you are made victorious in Him and given new garments of praise—royal robes of acceptance into His family. Putting off the old and putting on the new begins in your thought life and carried out through declarations and actions that are in line with your godly identity.

Signpost 11: Resist the devil and his Lies

"Submit to God, Resist the devil and he will flee from you" (James 4:7). The devil has already been defeated; don't let him bluff you. Measure his lies up against the spirit of truth and choose to believe what God says.

Station 11: Jesus Is Nailed to the Cross

The devil thought he could conquer God and take authority by having Jesus crucified. Instead, God has trumped death once and for all. As you submit to God and resist evil more and more, your old patterns are put to death and nailed to the cross with Jesus. As Jesus was pierced by those nails and hung there, He conquered the evil one who tries to pierce us with his lies and kill us slowly with "hang-ups." Through Jesus we are more than conquerors!

Signpost 12: Renew Your Mind with Truth

God's Word is truth, written by Him who is the way, the truth, and the life. We are transformed by the renewing of our mind.

Station 12: Jesus Dies on the Cross

It is precisely at that moment of death that the renewal can begin. There is new room for a new way, for truth, and for life. Just as dead vegetation and waste become fertilizer for new plants in a garden, so it is in the spiritual realm as well. Something is released when we lay down our old ways that nourishes the soil of our hearts and makes them ready to receive God's ways. Feed on His Word to keep that soil freshly watered and turned over.

Signpost 13: Receive Resurrection Power to Walk in Healing

God says that we are "strengthened with might through His Spirit in the inner man" (Ephesians 3:16). You now have the power to walk a different way, make different choices, and believe what God says about you. See yourself as the healed, cleansed, and redeemed person you are.

Station 13: Jesus' Body is Taken Down

Even before Jesus was resurrected, God's plan for resurrection was in force. You too can be certain of that as you move on past each dying moment, each attitude or habit pattern that is finished off at the cross. Again we have a dramatic contrast: never was Jesus so helpless in appearance as He was in death, His battered body peeled from the cross. Yet in that very emptiness is planted God's amazing power for all who believe.

Signpost 14: Redemption Becomes a Reality as God Works Things Together for Our Good and His Glory

There is nothing that we have done or has been done to us that God can't redeem. The testimony of a living, breathing, changed life brings a reality that speaks volumes and builds faith in all those who witness it!

Station 14: Jesus is Laid in the Tomb[22]

It is at the moment of planting in the earth that the promise of a seed sprouting is most real and explosive. In the same way, Jesus' burial in the tomb sets the stage for the empty tomb, His rising from the dead, and completed redemption. The way of the cross is full of paradox as life is found in death at every turn. If we humble ourselves before the Lord, lay down our own agendas, in due time He will lift us up (see James 4:10). Soon we will see the fruit of redemption growing in our lives, His holy agenda coming forth through us, just as it was from the tomb that Jesus burst forth with heaven's provision of redemption.

The Greek word for *redeem*, "lutroo," means, "to ransom."[23] To redeem in the natural sense of the work of Christ in redeeming men "from all iniquity," lawlessness, the bondage of self-will, which rejects the will of God, "who gave himself for us that he might redeem us from all iniquity, and purify unto himself a peculiar people, zealous of good works" (Titus 2:14).

In Sparkling Gems from the Greek, Rick Renner explains, "This Greek word *lutroo* depicts a person who paid a very high price to obtain the slave of his choice. Once the price was offered and

22. Wikipedia contributors, "Stations of the Cross," Wikipedia, The Free Encyclopedia, http://en.wikipedia.org/w/index.php?title=Stations_of_the_Cross&oldid=486485279 (accessed April 13, 2012).
23. *Strong's Exhaustive Concordance*, s.v., G3084, "lutroo."

accepted, that slave became his personal property. However, the word *lutroo* was used in another very significant way that also has to do with the concept of redemption. At times, a caring and compassionate individual would come to the slave market for the sole purpose of purchasing slaves out of slavery, to liberate and set them free. In this case, the payment offered was viewed as a ransom, paid to obtain freedom for slaves."[24]

Because Paul uses the word *lutroo* to denote the redemptive work of Jesus Christ on our behalf, it tells us several important things:

1. Jesus came into the world, satan's slave market, because He was looking for us.

2. Jesus knew He wanted us and would not be satisfied until the purchase was complete.

3. Jesus was willing to pay any price demanded to purchase us from the slave market.

4. Jesus purchased us with His own blood so we would become His own personal property.

5. Jesus paid the price with His blood, purchased us for Himself, and gave us a liberating freedom that can only be known by His work in our lives.

This means that the word *lutroo* in Titus 2:14 conveys this idea: "Who gave Himself for us, that He might purchase us out of the slave market to become His own personal property, yet He was willing to pay the ransom price to see us liberated and set free."

Jesus was born to shop in the world's slave market. The currency He used to purchase us was paid with His life's blood! The result of receiving this redemption and embarking on this journey into freedom is transformation! But we all, with unveiled faces beholding as in a mirror the glory of the Lord, are being transformed into the same image from glory to glory,

24. Rick Renner, *Sparkling Gems from the Greek*, (Tulsa: Teach All Nations, 2003), 63.

just as by the Spirit of the Lord. We are being transformed; we are all a work still in progress. Beloved, behold Him, look upon the wonders of His person, let His love consume you, for you will reflect what you behold.

Fragrance of Christ

All four gospels (Matthew 26:6-13, Mark 14:3-9, Luke 7:37-50, John 12:1-8) record the outpouring of extravagant love by Mary of Bethany. She washed the feet of Jesus with her tears and wiped them with her hair. Then she broke an alabaster box and anointed the head and feet of Jesus with the precious oil. Jesus said that what she did was a prophetic act, preparing Him for burial. She came away with the fragrance of Jesus on her. She smelled like Him. She had the glow of His Spirit upon her. The broken alabaster body of Jesus poured forth His very life, releasing the fragrance of His love. Just as everyone knew Mary had been with Jesus, may it be so with each of us. May we humble ourselves at His feet and be bathed in the fragrance of His love! Our identity will have the fragrance of Christ as we are transformed by the power of His love.

Chapter 7: The Courtship of God

As we were seeking the Lord's guidance for the title of this series, I (Shelvy) read back through the chapters and saw something I had not seen before. I saw a picture of how God courts one He loves. He is there at the very beginning, drawing us with His gift of life. We are God's own love-child, conceived in His great heart of love. Reading through the different chapters detailing various life stages, I saw the transforming power of that same great love at work throughout a lifetime. It was then I heard in my heart, *The Courtship of God*. I had never heard of that phrase before.

When I think of the word *courtship*, I also think of the old-fashioned term: *woo*. To "woo" someone is to draw that person to yourself gently and respectfully. Wooing is not stalking, not controlling, manipulative, or forceful. It doesn't demand a response from a person. Rather, the lover's passion is shown as much in patient waiting as it is in persistent loving actions. The lover's goal in wooing is to be able to pour out love and affection, but in a way that can be truly received by the beloved.

Where there is something real, there is always the counterfeit. In Galatians 4:17 (NLT), the Apostle Paul wrote of such: "Those false teachers are so eager to win your favor, but their intentions are not good. They are trying to shut you off from me so that you will pay attention only to them." Those false teachers tried to bring others into conformity with outmoded Judaic beliefs. Those kinds of actions are not respectful but pushy.

Each year, the advertising industry spends billions of dollars to "woo" consumers. It draws and allures us with claims and promises. If you want "the real thing," buy this beverage. Or if you want a little stronger drink, it's always served in a happy place among friends, where "everyone knows your name" and never at home alone crying in your beer. The promise that this candy won't melt in your hand but only in your mouth, fails to tell you that it might end up on your hips. A woman's desire for baby-soft skin is fulfilled by buying a particular lotion and proven by the caress of a handsome man. The latest cell phone is to connect us to loving friends but never to hear disappointing news that you've been fired from your job or that the doctor got your test results and wants to see you as soon as possible. The newest truck and sports utility vehicle will enhance any man's image and make him more masculine. You get the idea: lose weight, grow more hair to cover the bald spot, and win more money—then you'll be desirable, handsome, rich, and happy!

"Do not love the world or the things in the world. If anyone loves the world, the love of the Father is not in him. For all that is in the world—the lust of the flesh, the lust of the eyes, and the pride of life—is not of the Father but is of the world. And the world is passing away, and the lust of it; but he who does the will of God abides forever" (1 John 2:15-17).

I would venture to say that much advertising appeals to "the lust of the flesh, the lust of the eyes and the pride of life." I wonder if the scripture written about false teachers might also apply here. For many years, the TV has become the babysitter of millions of children. They want the latest toy seen in the commercials, or the cereal that they see advertised by "Tony" the talking tiger.

"For when they speak great swelling words of emptiness, they allure through the lusts of the flesh, through lewdness, the ones who have actually escaped from those who live in error. While they promise them liberty, they themselves are slaves of corruption; for by whom a person is overcome, by him also he is brought into bondage" (2 Peter 2:18-19).

We only have to look back to the garden to see that all sin falls under these three: the lust of the flesh, the lust of the eyes, and the pride of life.

"It was when the woman saw that the tree was good for food [the lust of the flesh], that it was pleasant to the eyes [the lust of the eyes], and a tree desirable to make one wise [the pride of life], she took of its fruit and ate. She also gave to her husband with her, and he ate" (Genesis 3:6).

So the world courts us too and tries to sell us a bill of goods. But the world makes promises that never deliver the satisfaction we long for. That empty place in our hearts remains void of real love and acceptance if we try to fill it with all those things advertised from that other tree.

How do we know what to trust? How can we tell the true from the counterfeit? How do we recognize the way God courts us and draws us unto Himself? And why would He want to in the first place? Are we just fooling ourselves?

He Dwells (Thinks) on Us

There are certain telltale signs. When I (Shelvy) first met Jim and I saw what a wonderful man he was, I thought about him all the time. I'd wake up in the morning thinking about something clever or funny he had said to me. I'd go to bed at night thinking about how handsome he was and how blessed I was to have a man like him loving me. That which is important to us is what we think about the most. Did you ever stop to think about God thinking about you?

"How precious are Your thoughts about me, O God! They are innumerable! I can't even count them; they outnumber the grains of sand! And when I wake up in the morning, You are still with me!" (Psalm 139:17-18, NLT).

Almighty God, the Creator of the universe thinking about me? It's too much for the mind to comprehend!

I confess that in the early days of meeting Jim, I wondered what he thought of me. Did he even think of me? What does God think of me? To say that His thoughts of me are precious is dear to my heart. And to say that those thoughts number more than the grains of sand I can't even count, which invade my shoes when I walk the beach!

The power that is in a love relationship can lift us up or can send us into the depths of despair. Love has the power to cause one man to give up a royal throne and another man to commit murder. Love can color our world like a rainbow full of promise, or it can envelop us in a black cloud of hopelessness. How I regret the many times I have grieved God's great heart of love by my wrongful decisions and actions. Forgive me, Lord!

So, how does the Lord woo us unto Himself?

"I drew them with gentle cords, with bands of love, and I was to them as those who take the yoke from their neck, I stooped and fed them" (Hosea 11:4).

This is real love—not that we loved God, but that He loved us and sent His Son as a sacrifice to take away our sins (1 John 4:10, NLT).

That We Might Dwell in Him

God is love. When we take up permanent residence in a life of love, we live in God and God lives in us. This way, "love has the run of the house," becomes at home and mature in us, so that we're free of worry on judgment day. There is no room in love for fear. Well-formed love banishes fear. Since fear is crippling, a fearful life—fear of death, fear of judgment—is a life not yet fully formed in love. However, we are learning to love and be loved. First we were loved, now we love. Not only does God draw us to Himself with cords of love, but He also pours forth so much goodness into our lives that it changes our heart and leads us to repentance.

God Woos a Dying Man

It was 2 a.m. and I (Shelvy) finally went home from the hospital at the encouragement of my first husband's night nurse. She assured me that they had given him something to help him sleep. With her promise to call if there were any change in his condition, I left the hospital parking lot and made the twenty-minute drive to our home.

I fell into bed from sheer exhaustion, and just before going to sleep I remembered a dream I had a few weeks prior: My husband, Steve, was with his longtime friend, Forrest, and they were having a great time praising the Lord. It's worth noting here that my husband had never been free enough to openly praise and worship the Lord, and this friend had passed away the year before. The Lord spoke to my spirit: *He will be set free to worship Me when he is in My Presence!* I felt God was saying He would be taking him home soon.

It was more than a year since my husband had received a fatal diagnosis that meant unless God divinely intervened, he didn't have a lot longer to live. He had never been an easy man to live with and now it was far more difficult. He blamed the doctors and me.

His denial was so strong that he believed we were all against him. It made no sense. Fear and anger were controlling him.

More than three months prior, the Lord had spoken to my spirit during a time of listening-prayer: *I want you to fast every Monday, Tuesday, and Wednesday until I tell you to stop.* He didn't say

143

why. In the past, I always had a specific reason for fasting. But I knew this was God because fasting is not my favorite thing to do; my flesh cries out against it!

While praying and fasting, the Lord really dealt with me. Attitudes and resentments of years past began to come up. The giant screen of my heart was playing all my sins in living color and it was not a pretty picture. For example, for years I would rewind the offences against me and replay them over and over, rehearsing the hurts. Of course, I was always cast to play the role of the martyr and my husband, the villain. Now, however, my self-righteousness was making me sick to my stomach. The Lord was cleaning me out in more ways than one.

Week after week, I would ask on Monday morning, "Do You want me to fast this week, my Lord?" And week after week, He continued to say Yes. I didn't like the things He was showing me about myself, especially in my relationship with my husband, who was becoming more and more difficult to live with. His fear and anger were running neck and neck for the most attention. His response to this illness in his body was to control everything and everyone. Steve was a man who liked to be in control, and now he had absolutely no control over what was happening to him. He stayed in denial most of the time, believing that all the doctors had just found another "sucker" to bleed dry, financially. All the while, he was bleeding internally and would have to go to the hospital and receive transfusions every few weeks. He would feel fine and prided himself on going to work each day, saying, "See, I told you there's nothing wrong with me."

I felt so sorry for him, but the verbal attacks were coming fast and furious. I was in survival mode, just trying to keep my head above water. The doctors had told me he might die from hemorrhaging and he would never make it to the hospital in time. So, every day when he left the house, I never knew if that might be the last time I would see him. If he was late getting home, I had visions of him laying in a pool of blood somewhere. The doctors also told me that this condition might continue for a couple of years.

God had repeatedly said to me, "My grace is sufficient for you!" (2 Corinthians 12:9). Just to make sure I got the message, He used His "saturation method" on me. Everywhere I turned, I received the same message. My older sister sent me a beautiful plaque with the inscription, "My grace is sufficient for you!" A friend gave me a teaching tape, the title of which was "My Grace Is Sufficient for You!" And another friend sent an encouraging note with "My grace is sufficient for you!" printed on it. And as if that weren't enough, I got in my car, turned on the radio to hear a minister preaching…you guessed it. "My grace is sufficient for you!" I threw up my hands in surrender to the Lord, "Okay, I got it! Your grace is sufficient for me!"

During those special days of prayer and fasting, the Lord brought me to a new depth of peace. A deep, quiet place of rest settled in me and my mouth was silenced. Just when I began to actually feel the sufficiency of God's grace, when I finally felt able to not only fast three days a week but also live under constant attack, it came to an end. On the thirteenth week, I asked on Monday morning, "Lord, do you want me to fast this week?" The answer came, "No." Steve had been at work for about an hour that Monday morning when his office called and said, "He is on the way to the hospital!" That was the beginning of the end.

The first Sunday morning of his hospitalization, I woke up with a dream: I was wearing all black clothing, and around my neck, I wore a long gold chain with my husband's wedding band on it. I recorded the dream in my journal that day.

Our friends and neighbors had been faithful to come and keep me company in the familiar waiting room for the Intensive Care Unit at the hospital. I could only go in to see my husband for five minutes out of each hour. That Sunday everyone would be in church and I expected I'd be alone until the afternoon. Much to my pleasant surprise, Susan Smith came, saying she knew I'd be alone, so she decided not to go to church but rather to come to the hospital and keep me company. Susan has been a spiritual daughter, loyal friend, intercessor, and is now a board member for Transformation Counseling Ministries, Inc.

I felt it important to be accountable, so I shared the dream with her. Much prayer and fasting had gone into trying to keep my heart clean before the Lord. I was weary from this battle and twenty-plus years of our difficult marriage. Was the dream from my own subconscious because I just wanted it to be over? Or was it from the Lord and He was preparing me?

Here I was, two weeks and two surgeries later, going to the hospital in response to the nurse's call. On the drive there, I recalled the events of the previous day. The doctors were making their early morning rounds. When they asked my husband how he was feeling, he replied, "There is no need to prolong this. I want everything unhooked, all these needles and tubes taken out."

I was taken aback. Steve had not said anything to me. I was surprised that he was no longer in denial but very much realistic. It seemed that all the fear and anger were gone and he was at peace. I sat by his bed as he laid his head back on the pillows and rested. After a couple of hours, he raised his head up and stared at the wall in front of the bed where a large number of get-well cards were posted. He said in a faraway voice, "It's so beautiful. I've never seen anything like it!" I thought he was referring to one of the cards, so I asked if I could get it for him. He said, "No, it's the fields, the flowers. They are unlike anything I've ever seen or imagined." I believe the Lord parted the veil and let Steve have a glimpse of the place the Lord had prepared for him to spend eternity. His breathing was labored but he had a smile on his face. He slept as contentedly as a newborn babe. I read and prayed as I sat by his bed.

Later, Steve woke up and started humming a little. He turned his head on the pillow and said to me, "The music, the music is so beautiful. Do you hear it?" I smiled and said, "I think the music is just for your ears." I knew the Lord was wooing him and drawing him to Himself, wanting him to be willing to enter eternity with the Lord.

That evening at the hospital, both of our children spent time with their father. He said to all of us, "I want to go home. Shall I go tonight or wait until morning?" We all said, "Wait until morning." We knew he was not in any condition to physically go home.

It was almost 7 a.m. that next morning when the phone rang and the nurse said, "You'd better come." As I returned the receiver to the phone base, I reached into my jewelry box for my rings and watch. In my spirit I heard, *You don't need to wear those wedding rings anymore.* So I placed the wedding rings back into the jewelry box. I picked up the ring I always wore on my right hand, my Jesus ring.

That early morning, entering his hospital room, I knew it would be the last time I'd see Steve this side of heaven. The Lord had wooed and won his heart. He went willingly. God had also prepared my heart so that by the time he passed, I was at peace and able to bless my husband.

The Lord's timing amazes me! I arrived next to his bed just moments before his spirit left his body and I knew my husband's time of pain was over. The physical pain was gone, but so was the pain in his inner man that he had carried for so many years. Only the shell that housed him was left; he had crossed over. The Lord's patience in lovingly wooing him had won out. Finally, my first husband was at peace. He was transformed by the power of God's love. His earthly journey was over!

He Chose Us

Every bride wants to be chosen. Of all the women in the world, my husband chose me. Me alone and no other. God, Himself, presented me to Jim and he chose me as his bride. Our heavenly Father set the example when He chose us to be His bride.

"Blessed be the God and Father of our Lord Jesus Christ, who has blessed us with every spiritual blessing in the heavenly places in Christ, just as He chose us in Him before the foundation of the world, that we should be holy and without blame before Him in love" (Ephesians 1:3-4).

"But we are bound to give thanks to God always for you, brethren beloved by the Lord, because God from the beginning chose you for salvation through sanctification by the Spirit and belief in the truth" (2 Thessalonians 2:13).

"You did not choose Me, but I chose you and appointed you that you should go and bear fruit, and that your fruit should remain, that whatever you ask the Father in My name He may give you" (John 15:16).

It is a humbling thought that God chose me and wants me for Himself. It isn't because I deserve or can earn His favor. It isn't because I'm so smart or have worked hard to serve Him. I bring nothing to the table but my sin. The Apostle Paul said in Romans 5:8, "But God demonstrates His own love toward us, in that while we were still sinners, Christ died for us."

Free Will

Free will for us is anything but free for our Lord. It is said that to the degree you love, to that same degree you grieve and experience a depth of pain. Our choices, how we exercise our free will, cost the Lord tremendously. Because God is love, He loves us unconditionally and eternally. He grieves over our poor choices, just as a parent grieves over the choices a child makes, knowing full well of the possible disastrous path that lies ahead for that son or daughter.

"'Come now, and let us reason together,' says the Lord, 'Though your sins are like scarlet, they shall be as white as snow; though they are red like crimson, they shall be as wool. If you are willing and obedient, you shall eat the good of the land; but if you refuse and rebel, you shall be devoured by the sword; for the mouth of the Lord has spoken'" (Isaiah 1:18-20).

"Willing and obedient" is like a hand and glove, a beautiful fit. What parents don't love that combination in their child's heart! How much more God knows what is best for us and what will bring us into our destiny! He wants to protect and provide for us. Jesus asks that we be willing and obedient.

Early in our relationship, Jim said to me, "It's evident that the Lord has brought us together." We both recognized His hand in the circumstances surrounding our meeting. A few days later Jim made this declaration to me, "The Lord has brought us together for His purposes and I'm committed to whatever those are." We had opportunities to minister together and the way the Holy Spirit flowed between us came so naturally, we knew God was up to something.

After some more time, Jim proclaimed to me, "The Lord has brought us together as a man and woman for the purpose of marriage and I'm committed to that."

As you may recall, my reply was, "Well, ask me!" I knew he was willing to be obedient to God's will, but I wanted it to also be his will. I wanted him to choose me, not because God told him to but because he wanted to. I never wanted to hear, "I only married you because God told me to." We heard another man tell his wife that, and their marriage did not last.

"If anyone wills to do His will, he shall know concerning the doctrine, whether it is from God or whether I speak on My own authority" (John 7:17).

We must choose of our own free will to accept the free gift of salvation. While Christ died for all, all will not receive His gift.

149

I, (Shelvy) remember a tragic weekend in August when I was ministering with a woman who received an emergency phone call from her cleaning lady. She had let herself into their home and found the husband dead, an untimely death. I drove the woman home and helped with the many things that had to be done at a time like that. When his distraught sister arrived, she spotted a postal package on the bookshelf. Through her sobs, she said, "He never even opened the birthday gift I sent him! And his birthday was in June," two months earlier. With love, she had selected a gift for her brother and had it shipped to his home, but he never received the love and caring that were wrapped up in that gift. He chose, of his own free will, to not open that gift sent by a sister who loved him. How sad!

While the free gift of salvation is available to all, not all will receive it. " How shall we escape if we neglect so great a salvation" (Hebrews 2:3).

It is our choice! God gave all that He had for our salvation, His only beloved Son. Jesus gave all that He had when He chose to suffer and die that we might live. Jesus is the supreme example of obedience to the Father's will. He chose to be obedient and in choosing obedience, God demonstrated both His love of the Father and His love for each one of us. It's interesting to note that in the center of the word "obedience" is the word "die."

"Though He was a Son, yet He learned obedience by the things which He suffered" (Hebrews 5:8).

"I can of Myself do nothing. As I hear, I judge and My judgment is righteous, because I do not seek My own will but the will of the Father who sent Me" (John 5:30).

When God gave us free will, it was a tremendous risk, knowing we could choose His will or we could choose our own. He gives forth His love—but what happens when we choose to rebuff that love?

Love Rejected

Nothing is more devastating and painful than to love someone who doesn't love you in return. Not only do they spurn your love but they brazenly run after other lovers. Such was the story of the Prophet Hosea. Award-winning author Francine Rivers, in her fictionalized account of Hosea, *Redeeming Love*, portrays God's covenant love for His people.[25]

God has made this same covenant with us today. "I will betroth you to Me forever; yes, I will betroth you to Me in righteousness and justice, in loving-kindness and mercy; I will betroth you to Me in faithfulness, and you shall know the Lord" (Hosea 2:19, 20).

When I (Shelvy) was growing up and I was being nosey, or my mother was trying to keep a secret surprise from me, she used to say, "What you don't know, can't hurt you." But of course, as a grown up, I found out that what I don't know *can* hurt me. God said in Hosea 4:6, "My people are destroyed for lack of knowledge." Hosea 4:1 says, "There is no truth or mercy or knowledge of God in the Land." Sounds like our land in this day and age.

While knowledge may begin with the head, in our intellect, it must find its way into our heart. My lifetime scripture is Philippians 3:10-11, "that I may know Him and the power of His resurrection, and the fellowship of His sufferings, being conformed to His death, if, by any means, I may attain to the resurrection from the dead."

It takes a lifetime and beyond to "know" Him in this depth and intimacy, and the wonder of Him will never cease!

Beloved, our God has covenanted with us. In His unconditional love that has no end. He has promised right living with justice, a love so great that it spills over into loving kindness, mercy, and a faithfulness that we can count on. He will never run out on us. On top of all of that, He says we will "know" Him. A lifetime isn't

---

25. Francine Rivers, *Redeeming Love*, (Colorado Springs: Waterbrook Multnomah books, 2005).

enough; we are to continue forever in the great joy of knowing Him! Beloved, He is a promise-keeping, covenant-keeping, never-running-out-of-love God! He says in Hosea 14:4, "I will heal their backsliding, I will love them freely." I believe the book of Hosea holds the greatest of love stories, God's great unconditional love for His people!

Love Covers

Love enables a sleepy-eyed parent to comfort a sick child in the middle of the night with words of love and assurance: "It's okay." Love enables a young husband in their second year of marriage to tell his wife she is beautiful—after she has lost all her hair to chemotherapy treatments.

Love enables a wife to say to her husband, "I choose to believe you when you say you are not having an affair" even though she had received a letter saying that he was. It would be almost a year before the truth came out. (The writer of the letter confessed that it was a lie and was written in a fit of jealousy over the success of this man. The confession came shortly before the letter-writer died.)

"Love suffers long and is kind; love does not envy; love does not parade itself; is not puffed up; does not behave rudely, does not seek its own, is not provoked, thinks no evil; does not rejoice in iniquity, but rejoices in the truth; bears all things, believes all things, hopes all things, endures all things. Love never fails" (1 Corinthians 13:4-8b).

His Love Never Fails

The setting was a three-day weekend for women in prison. She was a woman in her late fifties. I (Shelvy) first noticed her as she played the piano. Her hands seem to fly over the keyboard as if they had a mind of their own. Then I saw her smile as she sang with eyes closed and face tilted heavenward. As the saying goes, she was "playing for an audience of One." It was easy to see that this woman loved the Lord. As the weekend progressed, we had many opportunities to talk and it became evident that we were kindred spirits. She was a Bible teacher and mentor to younger women. She loved the old writers, such as Charles Spurgeon, D. L. Moody, and Andrew Murray. We discussed many titles of the old classics and found that we enjoyed some of the same books.

She shared with me that she had attended seminary with her husband, who was a Methodist minister at that time. As I observed her peaceful demeanor during the passage of that three-day weekend, it was hard to believe that, as a young woman, she had struggled with a severe temper—information she had confided to me earlier. She said, "With every fiber of my being, I now want to model to younger women a sincere example of the Christian life. I want to make a difference."

All too quickly the weekend drew to a close. As I began to say my good-byes to the women, I looked and she was right behind me. It was a long embrace as we hugged, and she said, "I'm so glad I met you, and I'll never forget you. Please pray for me."

With tears in my eyes, I turned to leave. The armed prison guards unlocked the doors to let me out, but she would remain where she has been for the past twenty-five years—behind prison bars. I never asked what her crime was, I didn't care. The Lord Jesus Christ has forgiven her. I comforted her with the knowledge that through His redemptive power, He has entrusted her with an unusual, but important mission field. Perhaps her life has touched more lives than it ever could have in her former church setting. His love never fails and His love covers!

God Sings

"The Lord your God in your midst, the Mighty One, will save; He will rejoice over you with gladness, He will quiet you with His love, He will rejoice over you with singing" (Zephaniah 3:17).

This verse brings such beautiful and intimate images to my mind. It reminds me of the loving relationship I had with my father. I saw him as my hero—he was six feet tall, handsome with black wavy hair, strong but gentle. Our family loved to go to the beach, and one of our favorite games was to jump the waves. Sometimes my father would sit me on his shoulders and take me out where it was deep and over my head if I tried to stand. I felt no fear because my father was there to save me if I got in trouble.

I remember when he would come home from work. My mother would be in the kitchen, cooking dinner, and she would call to us to pick up our toys and get washed up because it was time for Daddy to come home. We would see her comb her hair and put on some lipstick. We were all getting ready because Daddy was coming home. I don't remember my mother ever telling us we were to "honor our father" but she demonstrated it for us, and her actions spoke much louder than words. When he walked in the door, mother was there to greet him with a hug and a kiss. Then she would always say, "Bill, I'm so glad you're home. How was your day?" Then it was our turn, three giggling little girls, looking up admiringly at our hero and our "King of the Castle," who made us feel like little princesses. He was glad to see us and we knew it!

Little children are forever having bad dreams, waking in the middle of the night, afraid there really are snakes under the bed or a boogieman in the closet. That's when I wanted my daddy because he was stronger than anyone else's daddy. He would gather me in his arms and quiet me with his love. "It's okay, sweetheart, Daddy is here. I'm not going to let anything happen to my little princess." My tears would dry on his shoulder, as I would snuggle against the hardness of his chest. I was safe. His love was more powerful than all the bad in the world. Soon I was back to sleep and never even knew when he laid me back in my bed.

When I was a little girl, we would travel from Virginia to North Carolina to visit my grandparents. Road trips were a delight except for one thing—I would get carsick if I sat in the backseat.

So I was allowed to sit up front between my mother and father. Next to my father was where I wanted to be. Our family sang old songs together as we rolled down the road. It was so much fun. But the best part was being so close to my father, seeing him look down at me smiling as he would sing. In my memories, he sounded like a famous singer on the radio.

If an earthly father can give such wonderful expressions of love, how much more our heavenly Father can give: "The Lord your God in your midst, The Mighty One, will save; He will rejoice over you with gladness. He will quiet you with His love, He will rejoice over you with singing" (Zephaniah 3:17). God singing over me! It's almost too much to take in. It's like the saying, "I can look at God, and God can look at me, but I can't look at God looking at me."

As I described in chapter three, my parents enrolled me in the nursery department at our church shortly after I was born. It was in church that I learned songs about God's love and how precious I am to Him.

I believed in my head that God loved me, but it would be years before the message of His unconditional love reached my heart. Renewing the mind of my heart is a difficult task and only God is up for the job. "For as he thinks in his heart, so is he" (Proverbs 23:7).

So, I have a heart problem. It's hard for me to grasp the reality that God unconditionally loves me. *You mean He doesn't love me one bit more when I'm all confessed up, my performance orientation is in high gear, and I'm accomplishing great things for Him? And you're asking me to believe He doesn't love me one bit less when I'm in the middle of my grossest sin—what Paul calls "that sin that doth so easily beset me"?* I guess I better get it straight. Oh, the wonder of it! He really loves me, just the way I am, warts and all!

I could never deserve such incredible love. I can't earn it or pray it into existence. It's just because God is great! God is love. He can't help but love that is who He is.

When I was ten years old, I gave my life to the Lord. I knew what I was doing. My church said I was born again and I believe I was. At seventeen, I said to the Lord, "I'll go where You want me to go and I'll do what You want me to do." I just knew He'd ship me off to the darkest corner of Africa. I've been to Africa and I loved it and can't wait to go back. But on the day I really knew at a heart level that God loved me unconditionally, was when I was truly born again—again! I felt I had been baptized in God's liquid love! I felt saturated in its reality.

How did He do it? The Holy Spirit wooed me into new depths of surrender. Some might not think it was wooing, but remember that my free will needed to choose to receive His attention. Therefore, I had to come to a place of need and receptivity. I was in my thirties and was tired of trying so hard to live the Christian life. My efforts had failed miserably. As I knelt by my bed, crying out to the Lord for a power greater than my own to be able to fulfill all He had laid before me, I believe I received the baptism of the Holy Spirit. John the Baptist said, in Matthew 3:11, "He will baptize you with the Holy Spirit." I was unfamiliar with the phrase "baptism with the Holy Spirit" at that time. I just knew I was at the end of myself. It was almost as if I could hear the Lord sigh with relief saying, *Finally, she's given up. Now I can show her how I want her to live.*

As I cried and waited on the Lord, wave after wave of His liquid love washed over me, cleansing and saturating me with the reality of His love. For days after that encounter, it seemed I was on a honeymoon with the Lord. I had a renewed hunger for His Word. It was like the familiar passages were coming alive and speaking right to my heart. It was like reading love letters rather than a history book. I started getting answers to my prayers like never before. Previously, my prayers had been hit or miss and I would be surprised if something I prayed for actually happened.

I also had a love for people I had never experienced before. I had a constant reminder that Christ had died for everyone and that gave them immense value. What I did for the Lord was no longer out of duty or because that is what is expected of a Christian. Instead, my motivation was love! I knew He loved me and I loved Him in return.

I had received the heart knowledge that I was God's own love child. I was conceived in His heart and mind before ever being implanted in my mother's womb. I was supposed to exist, and it was in God's perfect timing. God has His purposes for the period of time He wants me to live because He knows the end from the beginning. This is not just my life that is special. God has ordained each life and has His special purposes for each person.

Even my name has been a blessing. After I got over wondering why my parents didn't just name me Shelby—because that was what most people called me—I began to say, "Shelvy, you know, S-H-E-L-V for victory-Y." So I grew up confessing victory. As I got older, I wanted to know what my name meant. What a joy to find out that *Shelvy* means "where God dwells." I've never complained about my name since.

"Oh, the depth of the riches both of the wisdom and knowledge of God! How unsearchable are His judgments and His ways past finding out!" (Romans 11:33).

Each new discovery has revealed more to me of this wonderful God we serve. He is so much more than the mind can comprehend. My spirit knows and hungers for more. A lifetime is too short. A thousand lifetimes is still too short.

"He brought me to His banqueting table and His banner over me is love." (Song of Songs 2:4).

Passion

Who can understand why a man would love, desire, and be passionate about one woman to the exclusion of all others? Why does he feel this passion for one woman and not for another?

157

This passion is so strong that it keeps the human population reproducing itself. With Christ, it's a love and passion so strong He laid down His life for His Bride. In our Father's love it's a passion so strong in Christ, He suffered and died for her. A love so strong it gives itself away for the other.

Do we dare to use the same word "passion" to describe what a lover feels for the object of his desire and for the agony and suffering of Christ? If you look up "passion" in the dictionary, you will find that its root meaning is suffering. Is suffering not also a strong emotional experience born of love? Is not love the common denominator in the experience of earthly man and the divine Son of God? Rarely do we see human love or passion willing to die to save the life of another.

In Donald Miller's best selling book, *Blue Like Jazz,* he writes: "God woos us with kindness, He changes our character with the passion of His love."[26]

Love Gives Gifts

I've heard it said that "you can give without loving but you cannot love without giving." He who is Love gives gifts to those He loves, setting an example for us to live by. The first gift I received from Jim was more significant than he knew at the time. The setting was a beach along the Connecticut coast. Jim and I and two friends were walking along the beach when Jim reached down and picked up an unusual looking seashell. He turned to me and placed it in my hand. Having only recently met, he had no way of knowing how much I love the seashore. When my children were young, I used to tell them that my little corner of heaven was going to be on the ocean. Over the weeks and months that followed Jim discovered that I love flowers, as do most women. Every time I came to Connecticut for a visit, he would meet me at the airport with a bouquet of

---

26. Donald Miller, *Blue Like Jazz*, (2003: Thomas Nelson Publishers), 86.

flowers. And every time I was leaving, he would take me to the airport and hand me flowers. I felt so special and loved. As I walked through the airport with flowers in my hands, people would look at me and smile. After more than two decades together, he still brings me flowers for no special reason other than he knows how happy it makes me.

When a man begins to court a woman, he wants to woo her. One way he does this is by giving her gifts as expressions of his love. These gifts are not empty but full of the overflow of his love. We talked with such a man recently; he was so excited to tell us about the engagement ring he had just purchased for the woman he loves and wants to marry.

How much more Father God must delight to give gifts to His beloved. First He gives us the gift of life. "Gracious gift of life" (1 Peter 3:7). Then He gives us eternal life. "For the wages of sin is death, but the gift of God is eternal life in Christ Jesus our Lord" (Romans 6:23).

The Gifts of God

"Receive the gift of the Holy Spirit" (Acts 2:38).

To study more about the gifts, read Romans 12, 1 Corinthians 12, and Ephesians 4.

We have different gifts, according to the grace given us. (Prophesying, serving, teaching, encouraging, giving, leadership, and showing mercy—see Romans 12:6-8.)

"Every good and perfect gift is from above, coming down from the Father of the heavenly lights, who does not change like shifting shadows" (James 1:17).

God won't take the gift back or away from you. God's gifts and his call are irrevocable. In other words, they are permanent! (See Romans 11:29.)

God has "hand-picked" gifts for you. He didn't call in His secretary to go shopping for Him. He has chosen you and He has gifts for you to help you fulfill your destiny. Have you received them yet?

"The Spirit and the bride say, Come! And let him who hears say, Come! Whoever desires, let him take the water of life freely" (Revelation 22:17).

The Journey

Our Beloved is calling us and will continue to do so. He has caused much to happen in each of our lives that would tell our hearts how much He loves us. He has drawn us with His cords of love. He has lovingly stepped into the circumstances of our lives to lead us on a lifetime journey. He evidences Himself as our Protector and Provider, Savior, and Deliverer. He is ever attentive to our prayers. He has lavished us with gifts and given meaning and purpose to our lives. He has promised never to leave us nor forsake us. He is always as near as the breath we breathe. His love covers a multitude of sins and His love never fails. We are altogether lovely to Him. Such is the Courtship of God!

Who can resist such a love? Who can deny such a Lover? He is the real God, and His promises are true. To be wooed by God is a high adventure: Enjoy the journey!

About the Authors

Jim and Shelvy Wyatt's Transformation Ministry began with their marriage In Israel on the Mount of Transfiguration in 1986. They have been in full-time ministry together as Christian teachers and counselors since then. Jim also achieved success in the corporate world as president of a nationally known consulting firm in design, invention, and engineering. Later, he became involved in prison ministry, co-founded Isaiah 61:1 with halfway houses in Bridgeport, studied at the Biblical Institute in Jerusalem, and was ordained as an Eastern Catholic priest (Shelvy as a deacon). He is a graduate of Cooper Union School of Engineering in NYC. Shelvy attended William and Mary College in VA, ministered counseling and teaching in Virginia Beach, and has been a frequent speaker at church groups, Woman's Aglow, CFO camps and Christian Woman's Club. They currently reside in Connecticut.

To contact the Wyatts for more information or for speaking engagements, please email: aetos7@att.net or shelvyjw@att.net

More Titles by 5 Fold Media

The Most Amazing Song of All
by Brian Simmons
$9.00
ISBN: 978-1-936578-03-0

Breathtaking and beautiful, we see the Shulamite journey unveiled in this anointed allegory. It becomes a journey that not only describes the divine parable penned by Solomon, but a journey that every longing lover of Jesus will find as his or her very own.

In this new Passion Translation™, the translator uses the language of the heart based on a passion for love to translate the book from Hebrew to English.

The Call to Peace
by Daniel Lucas
$11.00
ISBN: 978-1-936578-04-7

The Call to Peace by Daniel Lucas is the unfolding of the true meaning of the immeasurable "peace of God"- a common phrase among Christians, yet few really understand or experience it. Now, by compiling scripture, kingdom revelation, prophetic insight and life experiences, this book is the handbook on the peace of God.

The Call to Peace inspires the reader to answer the call to intimacy with God and discover peace in the midst of their own lives.

Visit www.5foldmedia.com to sign up for 5 Fold Media's FREE email update. You will get notices of our new releases, sales, and special events such as book signings and media conferences.

5 Fold Media, LLC is a Christ-centered media company. Our desire is to produce lasting fruit in writing, music, art, and creative gifts.

"To Establish and Reveal"
For more information visit:
www.5foldmedia.com

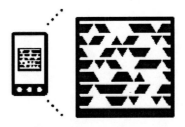

Use your mobile device to scan the tag above and visit our website.
Get the free app: http://gettag.mobi